MIDDLESEX CCC
On This Day

RICHARD "TRICKY" WEIL
MUSEUM

MIDDLESEX CCC
On This Day

History, Facts & Figures
from Every Day of the Year

STEVEN FLETCHER

MIDDLESEX CCC
On This Day

History, Facts & Figures from Every Day of the Year

All statistics, facts and figures are correct as of 15th March 2011

© Steven Fletcher
Steven Fletcher has asserted his rights in accordance with the Copyright, Designs and Patents Act 1988 to be identified as the author of this work.

Published By:
Pitch Publishing (Brighton) Ltd
A2 Yeoman Gate
Yeoman Way
Durrington
BN13 3QZ

Email: info@pitchpublishing.co.uk
Web: www.pitchpublishing.co.uk

First published 2011

A catalogue record for this book is available from the British Library.

ISBN: 978-1-9054119-9-3

Printed and bound in Great Britain by CPI Mackays, Chatham ME5 8TD

This book is dedicated to all those who have
been there for me, supported me and
have helped me to get where I am now.

For fear of missing anyone out and causing any
unintended disappointment or umbrage, I shall
refrain from compiling a long list of individuals,
however my most sincere thanks go to each
and every one of you who have assisted me along
the way, on what has not always been the most
straightforward and smoothest of journeys.

I'm sure if this dedication applies to you,
then you'll know who you are, and will kindly
accept my thanks for all you have done.

With thanks

Fletch

FOREWORD BY ANGUS FRASER MBE

Middlesex County Cricket Club will always be a special club, a county team that many people envy and even more want to play for. The club has a history that is rich and successful, a history that every supporter should be proud of. A county that has served its supporters and country well. Success has been achieved both domestically and internationally. At home only two counties, Yorkshire and Surrey, have won the County Championship on more occasions than Middlesex CCC and, as I write, Andrew Strauss looks set to follow in the footsteps of Mike Brearley and Mike Gatting by captaining England to Ashes success in Australia.

Strauss, Brearley and Gatting are not the only stars produced by Middlesex CCC. Its history is littered with notable figures. Denis Compton and Bill Edrich lit up Lord's after the Second World War. Picking out further names is dangerous because those I fail to mention will get upset, but the club has produced dozens of cricketers that have gone on to represent England.

I am proud to say that I was a product of Middlesex cricket. I did not represent the club as a junior but I learnt to play at Stanmore Cricket Club in north-west London. It is a club that my family and I are still very attached to. It was my performances in the Middlesex County Cricket League that caught the eye of the then Middlesex coach, Don Bennett, who signed me up in 1984.

The Middlesex CCC side that I joined was the strongest in the country and was winning domestic trophies almost every year. It contained eleven international cricketers – Slack, Barlow, Gatting, Radley, Butcher, Downton, Emburey, Edmonds, Williams, Cowans and Daniel – and was almost the Barcelona of county cricket.

Breaking in to that side was hard and for three or four years my appearances only tended to be when those named above were away on England duty. But the professionalism shown by these players provided me with great grounding. Working with and following the example set by these figures played a huge role in me becoming an England cricketer, and pulling on an England sweater for the first time remains the proudest moment of my life.

Ramprakash, Roseberry, Haynes, Tufnell, Carr, Brown and Johnson successfully replaced retiring greats and Middlesex continued to produce an extremely strong team until the mid-nineties. Since then the club has struggled to compete for major honours but the list of England cricketers continues to grow. Ed Joyce, Jamie Dalrymple, Owais Shah, Eoin Morgan, Steven Finn and Strauss have all gone on to represent England with distinction, and the club will continue to do all it can to serve its country.

There are many privileges that come with playing for Middlesex CCC but the biggest is playing at Lord's – the greatest cricket ground in the world.

Lord's is a place you never become tired of visiting. There is a special feel to the ground, a real sense that you are following in the footsteps of greats of the game like WG Grace, Donald Bradman, Garfield Sobers or Ian Botham, which of course you are.

There can be only one better feeling than leaving the home dressing room of the pavilion on a match day, walking down the two flights of stairs, through the Long Room, down the half a dozen or so rows of terracing and out on to the hallowed turf, and that is returning to the same room with a full house giving you a standing ovation for scoring a hundred or claiming a five wicket haul.

In my capacities as Middlesex CCC player and managing director of cricket I have been fortunate enough to cite Lord's as my office for more than a quarter of century and, even now, I never tire of driving through the Grace Gates or walking through the Long Room. It is a privilege, something no Middlesex CCC player or employee should ever take for granted.

Middlesex's cricketers have not only performed heroically during the domestic season between April and September, and this book will hopefully give you an insight in to the remarkable achievements of the club and its players all over the world, 365 days of the year.

Angus Fraser

ACKNOWLEDGEMENTS

A special thank you to Middlesex's managing director of cricket, Angus Fraser, for very kindly agreeing to compile the foreword for this book, his passion and commitment to the Middlesex cause are clear for all to see. Thanks Gus.

To the staff of the MCC library, my thanks to you for your assistance and for allowing me to reside in your premises on plenty of occasions, as I pawed endlessly through the archives when researching content for this book.

Thank you to the statisticians and scorers of days past and present, who have so diligently kept records of all matches throughout the years – without your commitment and accurate record keeping, producing this book, would undoubtedly have been a far more difficult proposition.

To the photographers who have kindly provided their images to the Middlesex photo archive over the years, my thanks to you, for your expertise in 'capturing the moment' for the images I have used within this book.

And finally a big thank you to those at the club who have offered me their support and assistance when putting this book together and for allowing me access to archive material, without which, this book wouldn't have been possible.

INTRODUCTION

When asked to author a book which chronicled in diary form the major events that have occurred throughout Middlesex County Cricket Club's long and proud history, not only was I genuinely honoured to be given the opportunity, but was also most intrigued and excited about the things I might discover when delving into the last 150 or so years of the great club I have the immense pleasure of working with.

I like to think that in my professional capacity of working with the club, my knowledge of events in the 'modern day' years of Middlesex is up to scratch, and that my knowledge of days gone by is more than adequate. Delving into the annals of the club's history however, searching endlessly through the archives, and pawing through endless scorecards from over the years, have exposed me to so many new and interesting facts, that authoring this book has become an extremely rewarding and enlightening journey. Furthermore, it has made me greatly appreciative of the many legends that have been fortunate enough to have graced the many cricket squares of England with the three seaxes of Middlesex proudly on their chests.

I guess, more than any other sport, cricket is a game of statistics, where the individual brilliance of a player on any given day can often be overlooked in favour of what actually appears on the scorecard. No one remembers the bowler who passes the bat endlessly yet remains wicketless, or the half a dozen chances a batsman might offer up on his way to three figures in the book. So with this in mind, rather than just compiling an endless list of statistics, I've tried to put them into context, to bring them to life and set the scene, in the hope that you can fully appreciate the efforts of those that feature within the following pages.

It gives me great pleasure to bring you this publication, which I hope will for many of you bring back fond memories of matches gone by, that you may even have been lucky enough to have been present at. Everyone has their favourite players from past and present, and doubtless I will have left some of them out; however throughout the club's long and illustrious history there have been some truly phenomenal representatives of Middlesex, and I hope that the facts I have put together give a good account of the majority of them, if not all. Middlesex players have shone through the years on the international stage too, so within these pages I have also tried to give a good account of their finest endeavours when playing for their respective home countries.

For the most learned of Middlesex followers, I hope this book brings back some fond memories and is representative of everything you love about the club. For the less steadfast, I hope you find this book to be a good reference guide to the key events throughout the club's history. And to cricket lovers everywhere, I hope you find this book to be an interesting read, and above all else I hope you enjoy it.

Steven Fletcher

MIDDLESEX CCC
On This Day

JANUARY

SUNDAY 1st JANUARY 1950

An historic day for the club, as the first Middlesex playing contract of one of the club's most celebrated players, Frederick John (Fred) Titmus, began. Titmus had played for Middlesex once in the previous season despite having no contract, making his debut as a 16-year-old against Somerset at Bath. His pre-contract appearance for Middlesex caused a stir with the MCC, who lodged a complaint with the Middlesex committee, requesting an explanation as to why Middlesex had included a non-contracted MCC staff ground-boy within their side. This prompted an apology from the Middlesex committee, who had now decided to offer Titmus a three-year contract. Many years on, Titmus became the most capped Middlesex player ever, and the only player to play first-class cricket in five separate decades for the club.

THURSDAY 2nd JANUARY 1879

Alexander Josiah (Alex) Webbe became the first ever Middlesex player to represent England at Test level. He was selected to tour with England to Australia, and played in a Test at the MCG in Melbourne which the Australians won by ten wickets. Webbe only scored four runs in the first innings and was dismissed for a duck in the second. Despite a hugely successful Middlesex career in which he made 247 first-class appearances, scoring more than 9,400 runs, this was to be his only Test cap for England. Alfred Perry (Bunny) Lucas, who was to join Middlesex in 1883, also played in the game, but was a Surrey player at the time.

WEDNESDAY 3rd JANUARY 1906

Middlesex mourned the death of a man who was instrumental in the foundation of the club, Vyell Edward (VE) Walker, at the age of 68. Aside from a distinguished cricketing career, which in its own right was exceptional, VE was at the forefront of establishing Middlesex as a county club and in steering it through the early years, largely bankrolling the club's existence. VE stood as Middlesex's first captain before handing the reins to his brother, ID Walker, after nine seasons. VE was noted for being the first Middlesex bowler to take all ten opposition wickets in an innings in a first-class match. VE continued his long association with the club after his playing career, serving as president from 1899 until the year of his death.

SUNDAY 4th JANUARY 1942

Right-handed Middlesex batsman Michael John Smith was born in Enfield, Middlesex. Smith played for Middlesex between the years of 1959 and 1980, forging a brilliant opening partnership with Mike Brearley throughout most of his Middlesex career. Smith played in 399 first-class matches for Middlesex, scored a total of 18,575 runs at an average of 31.64, and had a highest career score of 181, which he scored against Lancashire in 1967. Smith's run tally puts him in the top 12 run scorers of all time for the club.

FRIDAY 5th JANUARY 1951

A few eyebrows were raised when John James Warr received a Test call-up for England in 1951. Middlesex's captain in the 1959 and 1960 seasons was included as a bowler on the Ashes tour to Australia in 1950/51, making his debut in the third Test in Sydney. While Warr was undoubtedly a good county cricketer, he was not considered by many to be of international standard. Sadly the sceptics were to be proven right as no matter what he tried, Warr's bowling was smashed all around the Sydney Cricket Ground on his debut, finishing the match with figures of 0 for 142 as England were annihilated by Australia by an innings and 13 runs.

WEDNESDAY 6th JANUARY 1937

While undoubtedly one of the best captains Middlesex have had, Walter Robins will also be remembered for an incident that occurred when he was playing in the third Ashes Test in Australia in 1936/37 under England captain and Middlesex player Gubby Allen. Allen set a trap for Australia's run machine, Donald Bradman, which involved Robins residing at long leg, as Bradman had a tendency to not resist the opportunity to hook the short-pitched ball. It wasn't long before Bradman sent a skier down to long leg and Robins was duly waiting for it, but fumbled and spilt the catch. Upon apologising to Allen, Robins was met with the response "Don't give it a thought Walter, you've probably just cost us the Ashes, but don't give it a thought." Allen was spot on as Bradman went on to score 270 and Australia won the match by 365 runs, going on to win the series 3-2.

WEDNESDAY 7th JANUARY 2009

The ECB announced that Middlesex's Andrew Strauss was to be captain of the England national cricket team, commencing with the forthcoming winter series in the West Indies. Strauss's appointment followed the resignations of previous England captain, Kevin Pietersen, and England team director, Peter Moores, whose disagreements had become common knowledge and deemed detrimental to international success. Strauss stepped up to the captaincy on a permanent basis, having already experienced leading the side when deputising for the injured Michael Vaughan in 2006. Two years to the day since being appointed captain, Strauss lifted the Ashes in Australia after a 3-1 series win.

MONDAY 8th JANUARY 1844

The youngest of the seven 'Walker brothers of Southgate', Isaac Donnithorne (ID) Walker was born in Southgate, north London. ID took over the captaincy of Middlesex in 1873, after the resignation of his brother, VE Walker, and had a hugely successful playing career with the club between the years of 1864 and 1884. ID Walker played for Middlesex in 142 first-class matches, scoring 5,953 runs at an average of 25.33 and taking 151 wickets at 20.77. The 20-year reign of the brothers' captaincy of Middlesex, which had been in place since the club's formation, ended upon ID's retirement from the position in 1884, when he handed the captaincy to AJ Webbe.

FRIDAY 9th JANUARY 1891

The first eight Test series between England and Australia had all resulted in convincing England victories, and few predicted that this early dominance would come to an end when the great WG Grace led his side on a tour of Australia in the winter of 1890/91. His tour side included two Middlesex players – club captain Gregor MacGregor and top order batsman Andrew Stoddart. Having already surprisingly lost the opening Test in Melbourne, England needed to avoid defeat in this second Test in Sydney to keep the series alive. Needing 229 in their second innings to win, Stoddart hit a top-scoring 69, but England were bowled out for just 156. As a result, the two Middlesex men had played their part in history, playing in the first ever England side to lose a Test series to the Australians.

EARLY MIDDLESEX CAPTAIN ANDREW ERNEST STODDART

WEDNESDAY 10th JANUARY 1979

Middlesex and England captain Mike Brearley led his side into the fourth Ashes Test in Sydney, hoping to go 3-1 up in the series and retain the Ashes on Australian soil, having won the previous Ashes series 3-0 in England in 1977. Batting first, Brearley's men were dismissed for 152 on the opening day, with the Australians posting 294 in reply. Brearley himself scored 53 in England's second innings of 346, leaving Australia needing just 205 to win. A packed SCG crowd saw Brearley's England side knock over the Australians for just 111 inside 50 overs to win, with Middlesex's John Emburey taking four for 46. England went on to win the remaining two Tests to record a 5-1 England series win – the largest margin in Ashes history.

SATURDAY 11th JANUARY 1930

England's first ever Test match against the West Indies occurred in 1930, and included three of Middlesex's players at the time; Greville Stevens, Patsy Hendren and Nigel Haig. The Test was played in Bridgetown, Barbados and ended in a draw, with Middlesex's three players all playing their part in the result. Hendren scored 80 and Haig 47 in an England first innings of 467. Hendren again posted 36* in the England second innings of 167 for 3, and Stevens took five wickets in both West Indies' innings of 369 and 384, finishing with match figures of ten for 195.

TUESDAY 12th JANUARY 1864

With a general meeting set for the 2nd February 1864 to establish the foundation of Middlesex County Cricket Club, the provisional committee received confirmation from Mr Thomas Norris, the proprietor of the Lamb Inn, New Cattle Market, Islington, that his land could be used for cricket matches. He proposed three ground lease options: firstly, for £250 per annum, Middlesex would have sole use of the ground, with Norris upkeeping the ground himself; second, that for £150 the club would have sole use but maintain it themselves; third, that for £100 the club would have use of the centre part of the ground for matches, and the upper part for practice, but Norris could rent the ground out when convenient. The third option was agreed due to financial restraints, and this was taken to the general meeting on the 2nd February.

SUNDAY 13th JANUARY 1985

Middlesex's Mike Gatting became one of only three Middlesex players in history to score a double hundred when on Test duty for England, recording 207 against India in the MA Chidambaram Stadium, Madras. Scoring runs – let alone winning Test matches – is hard enough in the difficult conditions of the sub-continent, but Gatting's innings was all the more remarkable as it came in a convincing nine-wicket victory for England against a brilliant Indian bowling attack which included Kapil Dev, Chetan Sharma and Ravi Shastri.

SATURDAY 14th JANUARY 1933

During the infamous 'Bodyline Series', Middlesex's Pelham Warner, England team manager on the Ashes tour to Australia, was involved in a confrontation with Australian captain William Woodfull. The Australian batsmen had been bombarded with a succession of 'Bodyline' deliveries, with Woodfull himself being struck numerous times by ferocious deliveries from England's bowlers. Woodfull eventually lost his wicket, bowled by Middlesex's Gubby Allen for 22. A record partisan Australian crowd of nearly 51,000 were incensed by England's tactics and the atmosphere within the Adelaide Oval was one of complete disdain for the tourists. Warner went to the Australian dressing room to speak with Woodfull after the close of play and express his sympathies. However, Woodfull's response was reported as: "I don't want to see you Mr Warner. There are two teams out there – one is playing cricket, the other is making no effort to do so." Efforts to broker peace appeared fruitless, and England captain Douglas Jardine, who had a well-known hatred for all things Australian, continued to employ the controversial tactics throughout the series.

THURSDAY 15th JANUARY 1987

Middlesex's John Emburey had a Test match to remember in the final Ashes Test of the 1986/87 Australia tour. Not only had England already retained the Ashes, sitting 2-0 up in the series, but Emburey managed to achieve his best ever Test bowling figures and record his second-highest ever Test score in the match. In England's first innings, Emburey batted with great patience and resilience to score 69 runs from 168 balls, before taking apart the Australian second innings with seven for 78 from his 46 overs. Despite Emburey's heroics, England lost the 'dead rubber' Test, but won the series and the Ashes 2-1.

MONDAY 16th JANUARY 1956

Wayne Wendell Daniel, one of the finest West Indian pace bowlers of his generation, was born in Brereton Village, St Philip, Barbados. In a Middlesex career which spanned 1977 to 1988, Daniel terrified batsmen around the county circuit with his mixture of express pace and hostile bowling. 'Diamond' as he was affectionately known, was a fun-loving character off the field and was hugely popular with the Middlesex fans, in stark contrast to the fear he invoked in all who faced him on the field. In a brilliant Middlesex career, Daniel took 685 first-class wickets for the club at an average of just 22.02, with career-best bowling figures of 9-61 taken at Swansea against Glamorgan in 1982.

SUNDAY 17th JANUARY 2010

Middlesex announced that despite their best efforts to land the greatest batsman in the modern day game, the 'little master', Sachin Tendulkar, had reached a decision in favour of prolonging his international career rather than pursuing the opportunity to join Middlesex for their 2010 Twenty20 campaign. This would undoubtedly have been the biggest signing in the club's history, as well as a major coup for the domestic Twenty20 tournament in England. Tendulkar stated that he was extremely flattered and very tempted by Middlesex's interest, but said the Indian international fixture schedule was too congested for him to be able to accept the club's offer.

WEDNESDAY 18th JANUARY 1871

Financial problems blighted the club in its early existence, and membership numbers had plummeted to an all time low, despite the club having a no entrance fee policy for all new members. By 1871 the club had reached such a financial crisis point that a special general meeting was called and held on this day, which was to be one of the most important meetings in the club's history. Despite the main point on the agenda being the club's dissolution and its viability moving forward, only 13 members bothered to attend. In an extremely close vote, they chose to defy the facts of the accounts that were presented to them and voted 7-6 in favour of continuing the club's existence, so Middlesex CCC lived on by the narrowest of margins – just one vote.

TUESDAY 19th JANUARY 2010

In an extremely subdued and relatively low key annual auction – by Indian Premier League standards, anyway – only 14 of the players listed for sale in the auction were actually purchased by IPL franchises. One of the few who were, however, was Middlesex's Eoin Morgan. His stock on the world one-day stage had increased massively, and he was snapped up by the Royal Challengers of Bangalore for a relative cheap price of $220,000.

MONDAY 20th JANUARY 1992

Middlesex's Phil Tufnell recorded the best ever Test bowling figures in an innings by an England player in New Zealand, destroying the home side's batting at Lancaster Park, Christchurch. Batting first, England scored a huge 580 in their first innings before dismissing the Kiwis for just 312, with Tufnell taking four for 100. Following on, Tufnell then took seven for 47 as the New Zealanders were bowled out for just 264. Tufnell returned figures of 11 for 147 in the match and England won by an innings and four runs.

THURSDAY 21st JANUARY 1988

The club received confirmation that Nixdorf Computer Limited, a German-based international computer manufacturer, would become Middlesex County Cricket Club's new principal sponsor, taking over from retailer Austin Reed, whose deal had finished at the end of the 1987 season. Nixdorf signed an initial one-year sponsorship agreement, with an option to remain as the club's lead sponsor for a further two years – a deal they went on to fulfil.

MONDAY 22nd JANUARY 1883

The first Middlesex batsman to reach a Test match half century for England was Charles Frederick Henry Leslie against the Australians in Melbourne. England, under the leadership of Ivo Bligh, regained the Ashes, winning the three-match series 2-1. In the second Test of the series Leslie had reached 54 before being run out as England made 294 in their first innings. Australia were dismissed for 114 in their first and 154 in their second innings, losing the match by an innings and 27 runs as England squared the series.

MONDAY 23rd JANUARY 1978

Middlesex off-spinner Phil Edmonds recorded his best ever Test bowling figures for England while playing at the National Stadium, Karachi, Pakistan in the third and final Test of the series. Like the previous two Tests, this one ended in a draw; however, Edmonds shone and was well deserving of the man of the match award. In Pakistan's first innings, Edmonds bowled 33 overs and claimed seven wickets, finishing with figures of seven for 66. Playing for England alongside Edmonds was his fellow Middlesex teammate, Mike Gatting, who coincidentally was making his Test debut for England. Gatting didn't fare as well as Edmonds, managing to score just five and six runs in England's two innings.

SATURDAY 24th JANUARY 1987

Mike Gatting successfully captained England to victory over the strongly fancied West Indies side in a World Series Cup match at the Adelaide Oval, taking part in a triangular tournament which also involved Australia. Gatting played alongside fellow Middlesex man John Emburey, and few gave the England side much of a prayer against a brilliant West Indies side which included the likes of Vivian Richards, Gordon Greenidge, Desmond Haynes, Richie Richardson, Malcolm Marshall, Courtney Walsh and Joel Garner to name a few. England posted 252 in their 50 overs, before surprising everyone and rolling the West Indies over for just 163 to record a huge victory by a margin of 89 runs. John Emburey shone with the ball, taking four for 37 from his allotted ten overs.

TUESDAY 25th JANUARY 1994

Following the sudden resignation of Michael Sturt from the role of Middlesex County Cricket Club chairman, the club's general committee elected Robert Victor Charles (Charles) Robins to the post, subject to ratification at the forthcoming annual general meeting at Lord's. Charles Robins was the son of the legendary three-times Middlesex captain, Walter Robins, who skippered the side to the County Championship title in the famous winning season of 1947. Charles remained in the Middlesex chairman's post for two years before handing the reins over to one of the club's all time playing greats, Alan Moss.

SATURDAY 26th JANUARY 1946

Paul Wilson Brooks played just one game for Middlesex, but he is as much a part of folklore as any who have played for the club. He sadly died on this day in 1946, aged just 24, a victim of the Second World War. Brooks had been on the MCC ground staff and was an aspiring and talented cricketer. In 1938, he was ordered into the nets on the Nursery ground to bowl for the great Donald Bradman when the touring Australians were at Lord's to practice. Watched by the media, Brooks bowled a left-arm fast-medium delivery to 'The Don' which knocked his middle peg clean out of the ground to the amazement of all. Brooks received his first-class call-up for the final Middlesex game of the 1939 season, in which he made an unbeaten 44 against Warwickshire. He played just once for the club, without an average, and was unable to fulfil the great promise he showed.

TUESDAY 27th JANUARY 1970

Middlesex signed a little known pace bowler by the name of Dean Warren Headley, who was born on this day in Stourbridge, Worcestershire. Headley joined Middlesex as a 21-year-old and played for Middlesex for just two seasons, making 29 first-class appearances before moving on to Kent at the start of the 1993 season, where he went on to become a regular within the England Test side. He received 15 Test caps in all, taking 60 first-class wickets for Middlesex and 60 Test wickets for England.

THURSDAY 28th JANUARY 1869

After many disputes with the owner of the club's first ground in Islington, Thomas Norris, the relationship between landlord and tenant had reached breaking point. Norris consistently looked to increase the annual rental for the ground, and the final straw came when, in breach of his lease agreement with the club, he arranged a race meeting on Whit Monday and a fete the following day. An urgent meeting was held at the Old Furnwal Hotel, Holborn, where the Middlesex committee agreed that they should move from the Islington Cattle Market Ground immediately, despite this making the club homeless.

FRIDAY 29th JANUARY 1864

Following a meeting held on December 15th 1863 at the London Tavern, in which the official constitution of a brand new Middlesex County Cricket Club was discussed and agreed, a general meeting notice was placed by the acting honorary president, Mr C. Hillyard, in the leading press titles of the day, notifying all 'gentlemen within the county' of the meeting due to take place on the 2nd February, and requesting their attendance on the day. The notice stated the purpose of the meeting was 'to consider the report of the provisional committee, to consider the steps to be taken for foundation of the club, to consider the proposed rules of the club and to appoint appropriate officers.'

FRIDAY 30th JANUARY 1987

Middlesex's John Emburey recorded his highest ever One-Day International score in a World Series Cup match against the West Indies at the MCG, Australia. Emburey's innings of 34 came off 53 balls and included one six but, strangely, not a single four. Emburey's innings was not enough to avoid England losing this match, but his England side, captained by Middlesex captain Mike Gatting, went on to recover and beat Australia in the tournament final, making Gatting the first and only England captain to win a World Series Cup campaign.

SUNDAY 31st JANUARY 1864

With a general meeting due to take place in two days' time, and the new ground facilities in Islington having already been negotiated and agreed upon, the provisional committee received a second land offer from a John C. Deane, the General Manager at the time of Alexandra Park, offering the park up for use as a home venue for the soon to be formed county club. The offer was rejected, as it was deemed that having a ground at Alexandra Park would make the feel of the new club 'too parochial'. In retrospect, this seemed like a strange reason to decline the proposal, given that one of the stated objectives of the new club was to 'get together the best players they could, both amateur and professional, from all parts of the county, and to make the club as advantageous to men residing in distant parts of the county as to those in the metropolitan districts.'

MIDDLESEX CCC
On This Day

FEBRUARY

SUNDAY 1st FEBRUARY 2009

Middlesex County Cricket Club rebranded its one-day side, changing their one-day name from the Middlesex Crusaders to the Middlesex Panthers. The club felt that a change of image was required to embrace a fresher, more modern feel moving forward, and as such a new logo was created for the one-day side. Incorrect media speculation suggesting that the club had dropped its Crusaders name and image for reasons of political correctness following complaints from members was strongly refuted by the club.

TUESDAY 2nd FEBRUARY 1864

Middlesex County Cricket Club was formally constituted when approximately 75 'gentlemen' of Middlesex attended a meeting at 4.30pm in the London Tavern, and the club was officially formed. A Mr Beck proposed and Mr V E Walker seconded that 'This club be now declared established under the name of Middlesex County Cricket Club' – a proposal which was unanimously voted for – and the new club was born. Approximately 150 names had registered for membership of the new club, which were all approved, and it was agreed that any membership applications received prior to the 1st of May would also be accepted without any entrance charge. All officers roles for the club were appointed, with the exception of club president, as it was deemed that 'no candidate of superlative merits had offered, though the committee had been in treaty with several gentlemen.' Those present also agreed that from this point on, the home ground for Middlesex would be in Islington at the Cattle Market Ground, and the rental agreement of £100 per annum was confirmed with site owner Thomas Norris.

FRIDAY 3rd FEBRUARY 1995

When Middlesex's captain, Mike Gatting, strode onto the field at the Western Australian Cricket Association Ground (WACA) in Australia at the start of the final Ashes Test of the winter series, he became the most capped Middlesex player ever for England, playing Test cricket for his country on 79 separate occasions. Sadly for Gatting, the sentiments of his historic moment were lost on the Australians, as they defeated England by a huge margin of 329 runs to complete a 3-1 series win. Gatting himself had a disappointing game, scoring a duck in the first innings and just eight in England's second.

SUNDAY 4th FEBRUARY 2007

At the age of just 20, Middlesex batsman Eoin Morgan showed his true potential and displayed what he could do on the world stage when scoring his maiden international hundred for his native Ireland in a One-Day International ICC World Cricket League match against Canada at the Jaffery Sports Club Ground, Nairobi, Kenya. Morgan's blistering innings of 115 came off just 106 balls, including ten fours and two sixes. It was the highest score within the Ireland-innings total of 308, although even this was not enough to stop Canada winning the game. Morgan followed up his maiden hundred with another great innings of 94 runs off just 91 balls two days later against the Netherlands at the Gymkhana Club Ground in Nairobi.

SUNDAY 5th FEBRUARY 1899

Middlesex's all time leading first-class run scorer, Elias Henry (Patsy) Hendren, was born in Turnham Green, Middlesex. In total Hendren played 581 first-class matches for Middlesex between the years of 1907 to 1937, scoring a record 40,302 runs at an impressive average of 49.81. His highest individual score for Middlesex, of 301 not out, came against Worcestershire at Tipton Road, Dudley. In Hendren's Middlesex career he scored an amazing 119 hundreds for the club – more than 40 more than any other player in history – making him the only player in the club's history to score more than a hundred hundreds.

WEDNESDAY 5th FEBRUARY 1930

As a professional cricketer, there must surely be no better way to celebrate your birthday than to complete the first ever double hundred scored by a Middlesex batsman for England. On his 31st birthday, Patsy Hendren did just this in Port-of-Spain, Trinidad, against the West Indies. Continuing overnight on 155 not out, Hendren brought up the double hundred milestone on day four of the Test match in an England-innings total of 425, which set up an England victory by 167 runs. Hendren's innings of 205 not out makes him one of only three Middlesex batsmen to have scored a Test double hundred for England, alongside the legendary Denis Compton, who scored 278, and Bill Edrich, who scored 219.

FRIDAY 6th FEBRUARY 1873

Edwin Albert Trott was born in Abbotsford, Melbourne, Australia. Trott played for Middlesex between the years of 1898 and 1910 and is the club's tenth-highest wicket taker of all time. He took an incredible 946 first-class wickets, including his personal best of 10 for 42 against Somerset in 1900. Trott was also very able with the bat, scoring an impressive 6,253 runs for Middlesex at an average of 20.23. Bizarrely, having taken eight for 23 on his Test debut with a batting average of more than a hundred, he was omitted from the Australian Test team to tour England, despite his brother, Harry Trott, being the Australian captain. Trott opted to make his own way to England, joining Middlesex instead.

FRIDAY 6th FEBRUARY 2009

The second year of the Indian Premier League saw a number of Middlesex's successful 2008 Twenty20 cup winning side listed on the auction roster for the annual IPL franchise auction. In a frenzied day of bidding, despite the difficulties being experienced by the Indian economy at the time, Owais Shah was purchased by the Delhi Daredevils for $275,000, Tyron Henderson by the Rajasthan Royals for $650,000, and Dirk Nannes by the Delhi Daredevils in a pre-auction agreement. Murali Kartik continued for a second season with the Kolkata Knight Riders, who had bought him at the previous year's auction.

TUESDAY 7th FEBRUARY 1857

Middlesex's Alfred Lyttelton was born in the London borough of Westminster. Lyttelton played for Middlesex between the years of 1877 and 1887 and was one of the finest wicketkeepers of his generation, although he played only 35 times for Middlesex. In September 1880, Lyttelton made his England Test debut against the Australians, his first of four appearances. On his fourth Test appearance, in 1885 at the Oval, the Australians had reached an unprecedented 500 for six and England captain Lord Harris was so desperate for a breakthrough that he asked the great WG Grace to keep wicket, allowing Lyttelton to have a bowl. While Lyttelton had never taken a first-class wicket for Middlesex, his underarm lobs proceeded to take the last four Australian wickets, finishing with figures of 4-19. Australia were bowled out for 551, earning England a draw.

SATURDAY 7th FEBRUARY 1998

Playing for England in a Test match at the Queens Park Oval, Trinidad, Middlesex's Angus Fraser recorded the best ever Test bowling figures by a Middlesex player for England when he took eight for 53 against the West Indies. Fraser's wickets included the scalp of the in-form Brian Lara for 55. Aside from getting him a place in the record books, Fraser's efforts were in vain as England lost the match by three wickets. His figures, however, remain the best ever figures for an England bowler against the West Indies. Ironically it is Fraser himself who also boasts the second-best figures too – 8-75 at the Kensington Oval, Bridgetown in 1997.

THURSDAY 8th FEBRUARY 1951

Having made an 'inauspicious' Test debut for England in the third Test of the 1950/51 Ashes series, Middlesex's John J Warr was surprisingly picked to play in the fourth Test, at the Adelaide Oval, which finished on this day – as, it transpired, did Warr's international career. Having been smashed around the SCG, finishing with figures of 0 for 142, Warr was this time carved to all parts of the Oval, finishing with match figures of one for 139 as Australia won by 274 runs. Warr's brief Test career was over, but his performances place him in the record books as officially being the most ineffective Test bowler England have ever picked, with a Test average of 281.00 and a strike rate of 584. Warr was unimpressive on the international stage, but he was a hugely successful bowler in first-class cricket, taking 703 wickets at an average of just 20.75 in his 11 years with Middlesex. Unsurprisingly, however, he never played for England again.

MONDAY 9th FEBRUARY 1970

One of the all time great Australian pacemen and the world's leading wicket taking fast bowler, Glenn Donald McGrath, was born in Dubbo, New South Wales, Australia. Middlesex were lucky enough to have his services at their disposal during the 2004 season as a short-term replacement for Middlesex's overseas player, Nantie Hayward, who was touring in Sri Lanka with South Africa. McGrath managed two first-class appearances for Middlesex, taking nine wickets at 23.88, plus four List-A matches, taking three wickets at 42.66.

SATURDAY 10th FEBRUARY 2007

Middlesex's Eoin Morgan rounded off an amazing week of international cricket with the bat for Ireland in preparation for the 2007 ICC World Cup. He had already scored 115 and 94 in his last two innings before posting the highest ever individual score for his country by an Irish cricketer, smashing an unbeaten 209 against the United Arab Emirates in an ICC Inter-Continental Cup match in the Sheikh Zayed Stadium, Abu Dhabi. Morgan's record-breaking innings came off just 238 balls and included 24 fours and one maximum. Morgan's innings paved the way for a convincing Ireland victory, by an innings and 170 runs. Morgan's average over the week for Ireland was an incredible 223.50 from his three innings.

WEDNESDAY 11th FEBRUARY 1891

One of the greatest all rounders in Middlesex's history, John William (Young Jack) Hearne was born in Hillingdon, Middlesex. Hearne's Middlesex career spanned the period 1909 to 1936, when he was one of the most prolific run scorers and leading wicket takers of his generation. He amassed an incredible 27,612 runs at an average of 41.15, positioning him third in the all time leading run scorers list, and took 1,438 first-class wickets at an average of 23.16, also positioning him third in the club's all time leading wicket takers list. Hearne's highest individual score in first-class cricket for Middlesex was 285 not out, scored in May 1929. He compiled 71 hundreds for the county, and his best bowling figures were 9-61. Hearne also took an impressive 237 catches in first-class matches, the 16th-highest tally by a Middlesex fielder.

SATURDAY 12th FEBRUARY 1977

When playing for England in the fifth and final Test match of the series at the Wankhede Stadium in Bombay, India, Middlesex's captain, Mike Brearley, recorded his highest ever individual Test score for England, scoring 91 runs in an England total of 317, replying to an Indian total of 338. Brearley's innings helped England to a draw in the final match of the series, and England secured a rare 3-1 series win on Indian soil.

FRIDAY 13th FEBRUARY 2009

Middlesex announced the signing of 20-year-old Macksville-born Australian opening batsman Phillip Joel Hughes as an overseas replacement for spinner Murali Kartik, who was with Kolkata in the Indian Premier League. Hughes had only just burst onto the international scene with Australia, but he had done so with a bang, becoming the youngest ever player in Test history to score a century in both innings of a Test match in only his second Test appearance for his country. Hughes was an absolute revelation for Middlesex, scoring 574 runs, including three hundreds, in just three first-class matches, with an average of 143.50. He is the only Australian batsman to surpass Donald Bradman's efforts on his first visit to England. Despite Hughes's brilliance Middlesex won none of the first-class games he played in, and the club had to wait until their 10th game, in early August, before winning their first County Championship match.

TUESDAY 14th FEBRUARY 1899

Having already played Test cricket for Australia against England, one of Middlesex's finest players of his generation, Albert Edwin Trott, switched allegiances and played Test cricket for England against South Africa. On his Test debut for England at Old Wanderers Ground, Johannesburg, he took four for 61 in South Africa's first innings and then claimed five for 49 in their second. Four years earlier, his debut for Australia had seen him hit 38 not out in the first innings, 72 not out in the second, then take eight for 43 with the ball. Despite two such outstanding Test debuts, he strangely only ever received three caps for Australia and two for England.

WEDNESDAY 15th FEBRUARY 1899

Middlesex's Pelham 'Plum' Warner started an innings which would conclude in a brilliant unbeaten hundred on his Test debut for England against the South Africans at Johannesburg, helping them to a 32-run victory over their hosts. Warner, opening the batting for England, had made just 21 in England's first innings, but carried his bat through the second innings to record a magnificent 132 not out in an England total of 237. At the time, Warner's individual score was the highest score ever made by a Middlesex batsman on debut for England.

MONDAY 16th FEBRUARY 1948

Middlesex's George Oswald 'Gubby' Allen and his fellow team-mate, John David Benbow (Jack) Robertson, played for England in the second of a four-match Test series in the West Indies, at the Queen's Park Oval, Port-of-Spain which concluded on this day. With the first Test and this match ending in draws, the English were unexpectedly holding their own against a strong home side including the legendary trio of Walcott, Weekes and Worrall. The English team's success was to be short-lived however, as the West Indies won the remaining two Tests to secure a 2-0 series win. Robertson however acquitted himself well on his first overseas tour with England, scoring an impressive 390 runs at an average of 55.71.

MONDAY 17th FEBRUARY 1964

A Middlesex trio of Peter Parfitt, Fred Titmus and John Price were all included within the England touring party to India, and were selected to play in the fifth and final Test of the series, played over this day in 1964 in Delhi. Parfitt came out of the match with the most credit, scoring a magnificent 121 in England's first-innings total of 559 for 8 declared. India were made to follow on, having been dismissed for just 266 in their first innings, but dug in to ensure that this match, like the previous four in the series, finished as a draw. All three of the Middlesex men took credit from the tour, with Parfitt averaging 64 with the bat, and Titmus and Price taking 27 and 15 wickets respectively.

MONDAY 18th FEBRUARY 1935

Elias Henry 'Patsy' Hendren played in the second of a four-match Test series on this day for England in Bourda, Georgetown, against the West Indies, on what was to be his final overseas tour with the English Test team. Hendren posted scores of 38 in both England innings, as the two sides battled out a draw to keep the series level at 1-1, with one further Test to play at Sabina Park, Kingston. Hendren was once again in the runs in Jamaica in what was to be his final Test appearance for England, scoring 40 in the England first innings in a match which England lost heavily by an innings and 161 runs. Hendren's Test record of 3,525 runs from the 51 matches he played, at an average of 47.63, was equally as impressive as his Middlesex record.

MONDAY 19th FEBRUARY 2007

Having been relegated from the top division of the County Championship in 2006, Middlesex set about returning to the top flight immediately by appointing two times Pakistan national coach, Richard Pybus, who took over the coaching responsibilities from John Emburey. Pybus joined the club after a successful stint with South African side Titans, and was quoted upon his arrival at Lord's as saying: "I am delighted to be joining the Middlesex Team, and am looking forward to working closely with Ed (Smith), John (Emburey) and all the guys, in returning Middlesex to the top flight of English cricket." Sadly for Middlesex, Pybus left his three-year contract after just four months in charge, citing 'personal reasons' for his departure. A difficult working relationship between Pybus and captain Smith was thought to be a major factor in his decision.

WEDNESDAY 20th FEBRUARY 2008

Middlesex left-arm spinner Murali Kartik became the first Middlesex player to be purchased by one of the Indian Premier League franchises, when the Kolkata Knight Riders paid $425,000 for the Indian's services for the tournament starting in April. Alongside Kartik, Kolkata secured the services of Australian captain Ricky Ponting, West Indian Chris Gayle, New Zealand's Brendon McCullum and Pakistan's Shoaib Akhtar and Umar Gul. In total Kartik's franchise took their spending on this day to a staggering $4,825,000.

FRIDAY 21st FEBRUARY 1930

Middlesex's leading batsman of the time, Elias (Patsy) Hendren, became the first ever Englishman to score a Test double hundred against a West Indies team, scoring 205 not out for England at the Queen's Park Oval, Port-of-Spain, in the second Test match of the 1930 series, seeing England to a 167-run victory. In the third Test, which started on this day in Georgetown, Guyana, Hendren scored another ton, although his 123 was not enough, as England lost the Test match by 289 runs. This was largely as a result of the efforts of the West Indies' number three, George Headley, who scored a hundred in both of the West Indies innings. More than six decades later, George's grandson, Dean, would make his debut for Middlesex and later in his career for England.

THURSDAY 22nd FEBRUARY 1917

John David Benbow (Jack) Robertson, the fourth-highest first-class run scorer of all time for Middlesex, was born in Chiswick. Robertson made his debut for Middlesex as a 20-year-old, going on to score a phenomenal 27,088 runs for Middlesex at an average of 38.36 between 1937 and 1959. Amazingly, Robertson passed 1,000 first-class runs for the club in each and every season between 1946 and 1958, and went past 2,000 runs in nine of those 13 years. Robertson also received 11 Test caps for England, scoring 881 runs at 46.36.

THURSDAY 23rd FEBRUARY 2006

Work was completed on the new Mound Stand roof at Lord's, ahead of schedule and within the allocated £500,000 budget for the project. Eighteen years previously the stand had been fitted with a state of the art 'tented' roof, and the newly installed refurbishment continued this architectural design, ensuring that it continued to represent one of the most iconic structures in world cricket.

SATURDAY 24th FEBRUARY 1990

Having not beaten the West Indies in any of the past 30 Test match encounters, a record that stretched way back to the Trinidad Test of 1974, Middlesex's Angus Fraser took his first five-wicket Test haul for England, as they finally beat the West Indies. In the opening Test of the series at Sabina Park, Kingston, Fraser took five for 28 in the West Indies first innings and 1 for 31 in their second, as England won by nine wickets. Sadly the joy was short lived – the West Indies went on to win the series 2-1.

MONDAY 25th FEBRUARY 2008

England kicked off their winter tour of New Zealand with a friendly match against an Invitation XI at the University Oval, Dunedin, which brought England's Andrew Strauss and Owais Shah up against New Zealand's Iain O'Brien. Unbeknown to them at the time, the three of them would get to play together in the same Middlesex side in the 2010 season. Of the three it was Middlesex's Shah who shone, scoring a brilliant 96 in the England innings from 150 balls faced.

TUESDAY 26th FEBRUARY 1985

Middlesex could be proud that four of the club's players were selected in the England World Series Cup squad to play in Australia, but there wasn't too much else to smile about. Mike Gatting, Paul Downton, Phil Edmonds and Norman Cowans all played in the match at the SCG, where despite their presence England suffered a heavy defeat to a strong Indian side, losing by 86 runs. Of the four Middlesex boys, only Norman Cowans could take anything positive from the match, recording three for 59 with the ball. In a World Series to forget, England lost each of their other two group matches – by seven wickets to Australia and 67 runs to Pakistan – and finished rock bottom of the table without a point to their name.

WEDNESDAY 27th FEBRUARY 1980

Middlesex's Ian Alexander Ross Peebles died aged 72 at Speen, Buckinghamshire. He had an impressive Middlesex career between the years of 1928 and 1948, with his leg spin accounting for 610 first-class wickets at an average of just 19.87. After facing him at Old Trafford in 1930, the great Donald Bradman said of him: "When I got to the crease, I found Peebles bowling exceptionally well, and I may as well admit that for the first time in my life I was unable to detect a bowler's leg break from his bosey (googly). I watched Peebles as closely as I knew how, but there was no use. Neither by watching his hand nor the ball could I detect it, and definitely this day his bowling was too good for me. I had a most unhappy time."

TUESDAY 28th FEBRUARY 1989

Middlesex made a West Indies double signing, with paceman Ricardo Elcock and Desmond Haynes joining the club. With ongoing injury doubts over Middlesex's existing pace bowlers, Simon Hughes and Norman Cowans, Middlesex were forced to bring in back-up in the bowling unit, which came in the form of Elcock. Haynes was secured as a replacement for hugely popular opening batsman Wilf Slack, who had died suddenly and tragically at the age of only 34 the previous month after suffering a mystery illness. In Haynes, the club couldn't possibly have found a more fitting long-term replacement for Slack.

MIDDLESEX CCC
On This Day

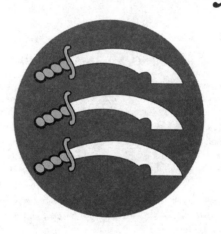

MARCH

FRIDAY 1st MARCH 1895

Bestowed with the honour of being the first Middlesex player to captain the England Test team, Andrew Stoddart led his side into the fifth and final Ashes Test at the Melbourne Cricket Ground with the series all square at 2-2. With the momentum in their favour, having won the previous two Tests convincingly, Australia posted a first-innings total of 414, before England rallied and scored 385 themselves. With honours fairly even, Stoddart called upon Tom Richardson to open the bowling in Australia's second innings, and he duly took six wickets for 104 as the Australians were dismissed for 267, leaving England with a target of 297 to win the Ashes. An innings of 93 from Albert Ward and 140 from John Brown took England to victory. Stoddart himself had a quiet final Test, but he had led the England side with distinction and returned home as a victorious Ashes captain.

WEDNESDAY 2nd MARCH 1977

Middlesex's opening batsman and England's captain, Andrew John Strauss was born in Johannesburg, South Africa. Strauss made his Middlesex debut in 1998 against Hampshire, scoring 83 in Middlesex's first innings. He has since represented Middlesex in 113 first-class matches, and has scored 7,700 first-class runs for the club at an average of more than 41. Strauss has also scored nearly 3,000 List-A runs for the club and captained the side between 2002 and 2004. He has 82 Test caps to his name, and made scores of 112 and 83 on his 2004 debut against New Zealand. He has scored over 6,000 Test runs for England, alongside 4,169 ODI runs in 125 appearances, and was appointed captain in 2009 following the resignation of Kevin Pietersen.

SATURDAY 3rd MARCH 1888

Francis Thomas (Frank) Mann was born in Winchmore Hill, London. Mann enjoyed a successful Middlesex career between 1909 and 1931 and captained the side for eight years between 1921 and 1928. During his Middlesex career, which spanned the Great War, he scored 10,654 runs for the club at an average of 24.60, including eight centuries and a highest score of 194. Mann made five Test appearances for England, all as captain, on the tour of South Africa in 1922/1923 – a series which England won 2-1. Despite this, he never played for England again.

THURSDAY 4th MARCH 1982

Middlesex's John Emburey was within a touring party of 12 English cricketers, 11 of whom had England Test caps, who travelled in secret to South Africa to take part in the first of the infamous 'rebel tours'. The tour was so secretive that it only became public when the England rebels touched down in Johannesburg. At the time there was an international cricket embargo in South Africa as a result of the ongoing apartheid regime. The tourists anticipated a small slap on the wrist from the ICC, but were stunned by the global outrage that their trip created, with the team being branded 'the dirty dozen' by MPs in the Houses of Parliament. Emburey played on this day for the South African Breweries English XI against a South African Colts XI side in a two-day match which ended in a draw. All players, Emburey included, received a three-year international ban for their actions.

WEDNESDAY 5th MARCH 1947

England lost the fifth and final Ashes Test in Sydney to lose the series 3-0 to a talented Australian side which included the great Donald Bradman. Despite the England side including Middlesex heroes Bill Edrich and Denis Compton, alongside Yorkshire's Len Hutton, they were resoundingly thumped by the Australians. The final Test finished in a five-wicket Australian victory, and it appeared that no matter what Middlesex's Compton or Edrich did, Bradman could top them. Edrich averaged 45.90 in the series, Compton averaged 51.00, whilst Hutton averaged 48.38, yet all were dwarfed by Bradman, who scored 680 runs at 97.14, including five scores of more than 50, one century (187) and one double century (234).

SATURDAY 6th MARCH 2010

Less than five years after making his first-class debut for Middlesex at the age of just 16, pace bowler Steven Finn was called up to the England Test squad as cover for the injured England bowling line-up, who were touring Bangladesh at the time. Finn travelled to Bangladesh to find that just a week later he would be making his Test debut for England in Chittagong following injuries to England's Stuart Broad, Graham Onions and James Anderson. Finn's rise from Academy youngster to England Test player is one of the quickest progressions through the ranks in living memory.

MONDAY 7th MARCH 1904

The fifth and final Test match of the 1903/04 Ashes series in Melbourne saw an England side, led by Middlesex's Pelham (Plum) Warner and including Middlesex's Bernard Bosanquet, 3-1 up in the series and already having reclaimed the Ashes after the lengthiest period of Australian dominance since the two sides had commenced rivalries. One can only surmise that Warner and his men hadn't yet stopped celebrating their series win, as England were resoundingly trounced by Australia in this 'dead rubber', being bowled out for just 61 and 101 in their two innings to lose by 218 runs.

THURSDAY 8th MARCH 1951

One half of the famous Middlesex spin twins, Philippe-Henry (Phil) Edmonds was born in Lusaka, Zambia. Edmonds formed a formidable spin partnership with John Emburey, and the two were instrumental in Middlesex's successes throughout a large part of Edmonds' career, between 1971 and 1992. In his time with Middlesex, Edmonds took 883 wickets for the county at 23.55, with career-best bowling figures of 8-53, making him the 12th-highest wicket taker in the club's history.

THURSDAY 9th MARCH 1978

In the final Test of a three-match series against New Zealand, played on this day at Eden Park in Auckland, Clive Radley scored a brilliant 158 to record his highest ever Test score for England. New Zealand batted first, and posted 315, before Radley's record innings took England to a total of 429. New Zealand dug in at the second attempt and reached 382 for eight on the final day to secure a draw in the match and in the series, which finished all square at 1-1.

TUESDAY 10th MARCH 2009

The final day of the fifth Test match in the series between West Indies and England signalled the end of Middlesex's Andrew Strauss's first overseas Test series as captain of England. England lost the series 1-0, but Strauss himself led the side with distinction, scoring three hundreds (169 in Antigua, 142 in Barbados and 142 again in Trinidad) in the England first innings of the final three Test matches, all of which England could only draw. Strauss scored a total of 541 runs at an average of 67.63 in the five-match series.

PELHAM 'PLUM' WARNER – THE GRAND OLD MAN OF ENGLISH CRICKET

WEDNESDAY 11th MARCH 1863

Andrew Ernest Stoddart was born in Westoe, County Durham. Stoddart was a fine natural sportsman, and remains the only person to have captained England at both Test cricket and rugby union. His Middlesex career spanned 1885 to 1900 and he captained the side in the 1898 season. He scored 9,255 first-class runs for Middlesex, at an average of 31.80, with a highest individual score of 221. Stoddard was the first ever Middlesex player to captain the England Test side in 1893.

WEDNESDAY 11th MARCH 2009

Middlesex unveiled the club's new principal sponsor, Ignis Asset Management, who had signed a three-year deal to appear on the club's playing shirts until the end of the 2011 season.

SATURDAY 12th MARCH 1977

Middlesex captain Mike Brearley had the honour of representing England in the 'Centenary Test' match, played at the MCG, to mark a hundred years of Test matches between England and Australia. Brearley scored just 12 in the first innings and 43 in the second in a game that England lost by 45 runs – which coincidentally was exactly the same margin of victory as in the first Test a century earlier. England captain Tony Greig was unceremoniously removed from his post two months after this game, with Brearley himself taking over the long-term captaincy. He captained England in 31 Tests, losing just four.

MONDAY 13th MARCH 1939

Middlesex batsman Bill Edrich holds the record for scoring the highest ever Test innings by a Middlesex player when touring overseas with England, doing so during the last ever 'timeless' Test match, the longest Test on record, at Kingsmead, Durban, against South Africa. Edrich's 219 was completed on the ninth day of the Test, which had started on the 3rd of March. Batting first, the South Africans posted a total of 530, with England scoring 316 in reply. South Africa's second innings netted 481, which left England a daunting target of 696 to win. At the close of the 12th day, with England on the cusp of victory having reached 654 for five, a decision was taken to abandon the match and declare a draw, as the England team would miss their boat home and be stranded in South Africa if the match went into a 13th day.

WEDNESDAY 14th MARCH 2007

Middlesex CCC announced that they would be embarking upon a unique charity partnership with the UK's leading breast cancer charity, Breakthrough Breast Cancer. The club announced that from the 2007 season, Middlesex would be celebrating the partnership with Breakthrough to such an extent that their Twenty20 squad shirts would be redesigned and the players would play in the colour of the charity's famous bright pink. This caused a few frowns amongst the more traditional of cricket followers, and some initial amusement within the sports pages of the national papers, but the club, its fans and the club's members took the initiative to their hearts and successfully help raise over £100,000 for the charity through donations and merchandise sales in the first four years of the partnership.

THURSDAY 15th MARCH 1877

His playing days for Middlesex came later in his career, but Australian Bransby Beauchamp Cooper played for Australia at Melbourne Cricket Club in a match that is officially listed as the first Test match ever played, when Australia beat England by a margin of 45 runs. Cooper batted at number five for Australia, scoring 15 runs in the first innings and three in the second. He goes down in history as the player who took the first ever catch to dismiss an England batsman in Test match history, catching John Selby for seven off the bowling of John Hodges in England's first innings. Cooper played for Middlesex between 1864 and 1867 before joining Kent. At the time of the historic Test match he was playing back in Australia with Victoria.

TUESDAY 16th MARCH 2010

Middlesex pace sensation Steven Finn made his Test debut for England in the Zohur Ahmed Chowdhury Stadium, Chittagong, Bangladesh, just a week after receiving a shock call-up to the Test squad to provide pace cover for the injured England bowling unit. Finn took two for 95 in a match which England won convincingly by 181 runs, going on to be selected in the second Test in Mirpur, where he again took two wickets, for 82 runs, helping England to another win, this time by nine wickets.

SATURDAY 17th MARCH 2007

On St Patrick's Day, Middlesex's Eoin Morgan was involved in the biggest shock result of the 2007 Cricket World Cup, and arguably one of the biggest shock results to ever hit world cricket, when playing for Ireland at Sabina Park, Kingston, Jamaica. Pitched as huge underdogs, Morgan's Ireland side beat one of the pre-tournament favourites, Pakistan, by three wickets, sending the Pakistanis crashing out of the competition in the group stage and giving Morgan's countrymen the perfect boost to their St Patrick's Day celebrations. Having won the toss, Ireland put Pakistan into bat and, against all the odds, dismissed the giants of world cricket for just 132. Kamran Akmal top-scored with only 27, and Morgan himself took two catches in the field. Ireland reached their target for the loss of seven wickets, although Morgan scored only 2.

TUESDAY 18th MARCH 1969

Middlesex's Shaun David Udal was born in Cove, Farnborough, Hampshire. Udal joined Middlesex having left the Rose Bowl and Hampshire after an 18-year playing stint. He played 41 first-class matches for Middlesex, scoring 1,170 runs at an average of 22.50 with a highest individual score of 91, and he took 91 wickets at 31.08. In List-A cricket he scored 410 runs at 21.57 and took 42 wickets at 32.50. He took over the captaincy of the club after the 2008 season until midway through the 2010 campaign.

FRIDAY 19th MARCH 2010

Middlesex announced that despite concluding lengthy negotiations with India's hard-hitting all rounder Yuvraj Singh, leading to him signing a contract to join Middlesex for their Twenty20 campaign that year, the Board of Control for Cricket India had effectively killed the deal by telling the club that they would not issue a 'no-objection' certificate that would enable Yuvraj to join Middlesex. With the ECB encouraging English counties to sign the world's best talent for this year's Twenty20 competition, Middlesex were hamstrung by the BCCI's refusal to release any of their players to the tournament, as were Northamptonshire, who had to issue an announcement regrettably stating that Virender Sehwag would also not be joining them as planned.

MONDAY 20th MARCH 2006

With the hosts leading the series 1-0, Middlesex's Andrew Strauss and Owais Shah were instrumental in an England victory in Mumbai which levelled the Test series with India in Sachin Tendulkar's back yard. Strauss scored a brilliant 124 and Shah, making his England Test debut, scored 88 as England made 400. India were then dismissed for 279 before England scored 191 in their second innings. This left India needing 313 to secure victory or a day to bat for the draw. It was future Middlesex player Shaun Udal who ripped into the Indian batting, finishing with four for 14 to dismiss India for just 100 and secure a brilliant England victory.

MONDAY 21st MARCH 1892

The first Middlesex player to go on a Test tour to South Africa was John Thomas (Jack) Hearne, touring with Walter Read's party at the age of 24. At Newlands, Cape Town, Hearne gave a good account of himself on his debut, although with the bat more than with the ball, scoring 40 runs at number ten for England. He also took one wicket in the South African first innings, for just 12 runs from his eight overs. England convincingly won the Test, dismissing South Africa for just 97 and 83 and scoring 369 themselves, to win by an innings and 189 runs. Surprisingly Hearne had to wait another four years before he received the second of his 12 Test caps, when he featured in WG Grace's 1896 Ashes side.

SUNDAY 22nd MARCH 2009

In the history of Middlesex women's cricket, there is no-one who has achieved more than their captain, Beth Louisa Morgan, who played for England in the final of the ICC Women's World Cup in Sydney, Australia, against the strongly fancied New Zealanders. Batting first the Kiwis struggled to recover from 92 for 6, to post a below-par yet respectable total of 166. In reply, England reached their target for the loss of six wickets to lift the World Cup. 27-year-old Morgan was run out for just nine in the final, but England had her to thank for being there, as her innings of 46 from 34 balls against the Australians in the semi-final was magnificent.

SUNDAY 23rd MARCH 2008

The third and final Test of the three-match series between New Zealand and England saw Middlesex's Andrew Strauss record his highest ever individual Test score for England. In a match that both sides needed to win to claim a series victory, it was Strauss who stepped up, hitting 177 in England's second innings to put England into a match-winning position. Batting first, England were dismissed for 253 runs before turning the tables. New Zealand were bowled out for just 168 in less than 49 overs. In England's second innings, captain Michael Vaughan fell early, bringing Strauss to the crease. He faced 343 balls and batted for 481 minutes to score his 177, helping England to a total of 467. New Zealand rallied in reply but were finally dismissed for 431, and England won the match and the series.

THURSDAY 24th MARCH 1892

The first Middlesex batsman to score a Test hundred for England was Andrew Ernest Stoddart, who scored 134 in England's first innings of the third Ashes Test against the Australians at the Adelaide Oval. England went on to post a total of 499 all out in their first innings, before dismissing Australia for 100 and 169 to secure victory by the massive margin of an innings and 230 runs. Stoddart received 16 Test caps in total, captained England on two tours to Australia and captained Middlesex in the 1898 County Championship season.

WEDNESDAY 25th MARCH 2009

In the pre-season friendly Pro-ARCH Trophy, Middlesex made it to the final against the Essex Eagles, played at the Zayed Cricket Stadium, Abu Dhabi. Their route saw them beat the United Arab Emirates in the Sharjah Cricket Stadium, UAE, by 110 runs before overcoming Yorkshire by two wickets in a closely fought game. In their final group match, Middlesex defeated rivals Surrey by two wickets to take their place in the final. Set a target of 236 to win, Essex reached it for the loss of five wickets in the 48th over to win the final and lift the trophy.

SUNDAY 26th MARCH 1916

Legendary Middlesex and England batsman William John (Bill) Edrich was born in Lingwood, Norfolk. Edrich scored a total of 25,738 first-class runs in 389 matches for the county at an average of 43.40 between the years of 1937 and 1958, with a highest score of 267 not out. Edrich is the fifth-highest first-class run scorer in the club's history and has 62 hundreds to his name. Known predominantly for his batting, Edrich also took an impressive 328 wickets for the club at just 30.41, with best bowling figures of 7 for 48 to his name.

MONDAY 27th MARCH 2006

During a Middlesex career which spanned the years of 1982 and 1994, Neil Williams, or Nelly as he was better known, played through the Brearley/Gatting era – arguably the most successful extended period in the club's history. Williams played 193 first-class matches and 197 List-A matches for Middlesex and was, quoting his first Middlesex captain, Mike Brearley, "a modest and unassuming person, who always did his absolute best for the team". The club mourned the death of Williams on this day, who suddenly and tragically died of pneumonia, three weeks after suffering a stroke in his native home country of St Vincent in the Caribbean. Williams' services to Middlesex are marked by a commemorative bench, which sits today within the Coronation Gardens at Lord's.

SUNDAY 28th MARCH 2010

Middlesex's season plans were thrown into turmoil when the club heard that the world-class experienced South African pace bowler Makhaya Ntini would not be joining the club as a Kolpak player for the season ahead, despite the club having a signed contract from the player in their hands since the previous October and receiving confirmation that he would be joining the club. Ultimately, Ntini's u-turn on joining Middlesex in favour of continuing to represent South Africa at international level was influenced by the South African Cricket Board issuing him with a tier two central contract, despite him confirming that he was looking to retire from international cricket. Ironically, Ntini never even got to play for South Africa again in any form of international fixture, retiring from international cricket later in the year.

WEDNESDAY 29th MARCH 1922

A sad day in the club's history as, at the age of 80, the last remaining brother of the famous seven Walker brothers of Southgate, Russell Donnithorne Walker, passed away. RD Walker was the club's president until the day he died, having taken over from his brother VE Walker. So ended the relationship between the original seven Walker brothers, who had been so instrumental in the development and survival of the club in its early days. There is no direct association between Middlesex and the Walker family today, but much is owed to them, and it is fitting that Middlesex continue to play occasional matches at Southgate Cricket Club's Walker Ground, which is named after the family.

WEDNESDAY 30th MARCH 1994

On a day that Middlesex's Angus Fraser and the rest of his England Test teammates would probably rather forget, their England Test side were dismissed in the quickest time in the history of Test cricket in Port-of-Spain, Trinidad. It took the West Indies side, including Courtney Walsh and Curtly Ambrose, just 19.1 overs to dismiss the England side for 46, their second-lowest Test total ever, and England lost the match by 147 runs. At least Angus Fraser could hold his head high, as he remained the not out batsman in the England innings, although I suspect this offered him little consolation.

WEDNESDAY 31st MARCH 1993

At a Middlesex general committee meeting it was agreed that a memorial headstone should be purchased at the club's expense and erected at the resting place of one of Middlesex's most legendary players. Albert Edwin Trott died in 1914, committing suicide by firearm after falling into considerable financial difficulty. Middlesex held a benefit match in Trott's honour at Lord's in 1907, in which Trott himself stole the headlines by taking four wickets in four balls, then taking a second hat-trick in the same innings. Ironically, the early end to the game significantly impacted on his own benefit match income, leading him to declare that he had "bowled himself into the poor house". Trott is buried in Willesden Cemetery, where the headstone erected by Middlesex, inscribed with the words "Albert Edwin Trott, 1873 – 1914, A Great Cricketer. Australia, Middlesex and England" remains today.

MIDDLESEX CCC
On This Day

APRIL

MONDAY 1st APRIL 1935

One of the most stylish wicketkeepers the game has ever seen, John Thomas (JT) Murray, was born in North Kensington, London. Murray played more than 500 first-class matches for Middlesex, having made his debut as a 17-year-old. In a Middlesex career which ran between 1952 and 1975, he scored 15,251 runs at an average of 23.24, which puts him in the top 15 run scorers of all time for the club. His highest individual score with the bat was 133*. It was his glove work that made him one of the best of all time however, claiming 1,024 catches behind the stumps and making 200 stumpings. Murray is the leading victim taker of all time for Middlesex and the only wicketkeeper to have more than 1,000 dismissals to his name.

WEDNESDAY 2nd APRIL 2008

Following complications with the ECB over the registration of Middlesex's intended signing, South African Friedel de Wet, the club instead announced the signing of Dirk Peter Nannes for the 2008 season. At the time, Nannes joined Middlesex as a relatively unknown cricketer, with little celebration coming upon his his arrival at the club. This would soon change, as Nannes set the world alight with his blistering 90 mph+ pace and accurate late swinging deliveries, and was instrumental in Middlesex winning the Twenty20 cup that year. Nannes took 43 wickets in total for Middlesex in the season, including a brilliant hat-trick at Chelmsford against Essex in the Twenty20 cup. Nannes was an interesting character, having previously been an alpine World Cup skier, and was dual-qualified to play cricket for both the Netherlands and Australia.

THURSDAY 3rd APRIL 1930

When England began their first innings of the fourth match of the 1930/1931 Test series against the West Indies at Sabina Park, Kingston, Jamaica, few could have predicted that the English side would bat on for two and a half days and post their highest ever Test match-innings total on foreign soil. The England side included both Patsy Hendren and Nigel Haig of Middlesex, who managed to score 61 and 28 respectively in the huge total of 849 all out from a total of 258.2 overs. Surprisingly, despite the record total, the match ended in a draw.

THURSDAY 4th APRIL 1957

Middlesex's leading victim taker in List-A cricket, wicketkeeper Paul Rupert Downton, was born in Farnborough, Kent. Downton joined the club from Kent, making his debut for Middlesex in the season of 1980. In a Middlesex career that was cut short after Downton was freakishly injured by being struck in the eye by a flying bail while standing up to the stumps, he took a club record of 259 List-A dismissals for Middlesex as a wicketkeeper, as well as 546 first-class dismissals – the fifth-highest in the club's history. Downton represented England at Test level on 30 occasions, taking 70 catches and 5 stumpings, and took 26 catches and 3 stumpings in the 28 One-Day Internationals he played for his country.

TUESDAY 4th APRIL 1989

Middlesex and England pace bowler Steven Thomas Finn was born in Watford, Hertfordshire. Finn joined the Middlesex Academy in Finchley as a youngster and progressed rapidly through the Middlesex playing ranks, from Middlesex second XI to earning an England Test cap in less than five years. Finn made his first-class debut aged just 16 in June 2005 against the Cambridge University Centre of Cricketing Excellence at Fenner's Ground, Cambridge, returning match figures of 2-53. On his County Championship debut against Gloucestershire in September 2007 he took five for 72 in the match. He has since made 38 first-class appearances for Middlesex, with best bowling figures of nine for 37 and best match figures of 14 for 106, both against Worcestershire at New Road in April 2010. He earned an England Test call up in early 2010 and made his debut against Bangladesh in Chittagong in March 2010 and has taken 46 Test wickets in just 11 Test matches.

WEDNESDAY 5th APRIL 2006

Middlesex announce that John Emburey is appointed to the new role of the club's director of cricket, a position which would not only see him take on the first XI coaching responsibilities, but also overseeing the management of cricket at all levels within the club. After an impressive Middlesex playing career spanning nearly two and a half decades, and with a deep passion for all things Middlesex cricket, Emburey was seen as the perfect appointment for the new role.

TUESDAY 6th APRIL 2010

Middlesex announce the signing of Australia's hard-hitting Twenty20 specialist, David Andrew Warner. Warner had burst onto the international cricket scene by smashing 89 runs off just 64 balls against South Africa on his international Twenty20 debut, and joined the club for the entire domestic 2010 Twenty20 campaign. In the week that Warner was announced as Middlesex's new signing, he scored a phenomenal 107 not out off just 69 balls for the Delhi Daredevils in the Indian Premier League. Warner didn't perform to his potential, however, rarely setting the world alight when playing for Middlesex. In all, he scored 268 runs for Middlesex in 13 innings, at a disappointing average of just 20.61.

TUESDAY 7th APRIL 1987

Playing in the One-Day International Sharjah Cup in the Sharjah Cricket Association Stadium, Middlesex's John Emburey captained the England side to a victory over the much-fancied Pakistanis, captained by Imran Khan. Winning the toss, Emburey put Pakistan in to bat, and England duly restricted them to just 217 from their 50 overs, with Emburey himself picking up the wicket of Saleem Yousuf. England's reply started terribly as Graham Gooch was dismissed for just one, but England soon got going and reached the winning target in the 48th over, with Emburey fittingly being in at the end to see England over the line. England went on to beat Australia in their next match, which was enough to put them at the top of the table and allow Emburey to lift the Sharjah Cup.

THURSDAY 8th APRIL 1965

One of the key components of Middlesex's back-to-back Championship-winning sides of 1920 and 1921, Frederick John (Jack) Durston passed away on this day in Southall, Middlesex. Durston took more than one hundred wickets in both Championship-winning seasons, and took nearly 1,200 first-class wickets for the club between 1919 and 1933. He was unlucky to have only been given one Test cap by England, which he earned after taking 11 wickets for the MCC against Warwick Armstrong's famously strong Australian team when they toured England in 1921. He was duly called up to the Test side for the second Test against Australia, in which he took five for 136 at Lord's on debut, but he never played for his country again.

FRIDAY 9th APRIL 2010

One of the most promising youngsters to ever progress through the Middlesex Academy, Steven Thomas Finn, had the game of his life in the 2010 season opener. At New Road against Worcestershire, Finn claimed five Worcestershire wickets for 69 runs in the first innings, which he followed up with nine wickets in the second innings for just 37 runs to return first-class career-best match figures of 14 for 106. Despite Finn's amazing performance, where he claimed the best Middlesex bowling figures since 1977, Middlesex lost the match to Worcestershire by 111 runs.

SUNDAY 10th APRIL 1994

Under the leadership of England captain Michael Atherton, Middlesex's Angus Fraser, Mark Ramprakash and Philip Tufnell all played in the fourth Test match of a five-match series in the Caribbean at Bridgetown, Barbados. Already 3-0 down in the series, the England side had little more than pride to play for, a quality Fraser showed in abundance. He took all but two of the West Indies first innings wickets as the home side were bowled out for 304 in reply to England's total of 355. Fraser finished the innings with figures of eight for 75 from 28.5 overs. After England declared on 394 for seven in their second innings, the West Indies were dismissed for just 237, and England wrapped up a win in the fourth Test. Tufnell's figures in the second innings were three for 100, with one of the wickets being that of his old Middlesex teammate, Desmond Haynes.

TUESDAY 11th APRIL 1995

With SmithKline Beecham's principal sponsorship ending at the end of 1994, the club had yet to secure a main sponsor for the 1995 season and onwards. At the 11th hour, with the season just a couple of weeks away, the club secured a new one-year principal sponsorship agreement with multinational consumer electronics group Panasonic. The initial deal was put together at very short notice, with the intention of solving the club's financial problem of going into the 1995 season without a lead sponsor, but it was hoped that the deal would prove more financially beneficial to the club over a longer period.

FRIDAY 12th APRIL 1991

The Middlesex committee received their first sight of a new proposal, put together by the cricket committee of the TCCB, entitled 'RAL 1992 and Beyond' – a report outlining a radical overhaul of the format and appearance of the domestic one-day competition, the Refuge Assurance League. It included, among other things, a proposal that first-class counties would have to ditch their traditional whites and play in coloured clothing. Not surprisingly this suggestion was met with dismay from the majority of cricket committees, whose backgrounds edged more towards the traditional than the forward-thinking. As such, the Middlesex committee set up a working party with the purpose of closely studying "the question of coloured clothing".

SUNDAY 13th APRIL 1986

Day three of the final Test match of an England tour to the West Indies took place on this day in Antigua, with England looking to avoid defeat and the humiliation of a 5-0 series defeat. Four Middlesex men, Mike Gatting, John Emburey, Paul Downton and Phil Edmonds, were all selected in the Test squad that toured the Caribbean under David Gower in 1985/86 in a series to forget. They could do little to stop the dominant West Indies repeating the whitewash they had achieved on English soil just two years earlier, which the media had dubbed the 'blackwash series'. Gatting played in just one of the five Tests due to injury, scoring just 15 and one. Downton played in all five, but managed to score only 91 runs. Emburey played in four and managed to score just 64 runs and take only 14 wickets. Edmonds played in three, scoring just 36 runs and taking only 3 wickets. Losing the final Test in Antigua saw David Gower claim the unenviable record as captain of losing ten straight Test matches to the West Indies.

SATURDAY 14th APRIL 1990

Opening batsman Desmond Haynes scored his highest ever first-class innings when he made 255 not out against Sussex at Lord's. Haynes's innings helped Middlesex to a first-innings total of 449 for eight declared, which Sussex replied to with 387 in their own first innings to ensure that a draw was the only result possible in the match.

SATURDAY 14th APRIL 2007

Middlesex's captain, Ed Smith, started the 2007 season with an unbeaten hundred in Middlesex's first innings, scoring 149 not out against the Oxford University of Cricketing Excellence at the University Parks in Oxford. Smith's season went from strength to strength, and finished as his best on record for Middlesex, scoring five first-class centuries on his way to 1,219 runs and an average of 58.04. Smith led the side to third in the second division of the County Championship table, missing out on promotion by just one place despite losing only two games during the entire season. Defeat in Middlesex's final match of the season to Essex condemned the club to another season in the second tier.

WEDNESDAY 15th APRIL 2009

Close to 300 members attended Middlesex's annual general meeting in the Thomas Lord Suite at Lord's, as high on the agenda was a vote to abolish the club's existing general committee structure – an administrative system of running the club which had been in place since the club's formation 145 years beforehand – in favour of a more streamlined executive board structure. The Middlesex members voted in unanimous majority for the change, which saw the club's existing committee of 18 elected members downsized to just 11, with a new executive board structure aiming to modernise the club and move it forward.

WEDNESDAY 16th APRIL 2008

While the opening County Championship fixture of Middlesex's 2008 season started badly for the club, losing to Leicestershire at Grace Road by six wickets, the season kicked off in fine fashion for Owais Shah. In Middlesex's first innings he scored 116 runs, which he followed up with a patient 50 in the second innings. Shah's brilliant start to the season saw him score 1,012 first-class runs for Middlesex in 2008 at an average of 42.16, and was the eighth successive season he had reached 1,000 runs. This, however, was the last season in which he managed the feat, and his form declined after 2008, leading to him leaving Middlesex after the 2010 season to join Essex. Shah left Middlesex having scored more than 13,000 first-class runs for the club. He should undoubtedly have received more international appearances as reward for his consistency for Middlesex.

MONDAY 17th APRIL 1961

In Enfield, St Mary, Jamaica, Norman George Cowans was born, before moving with his family to England as an 11-year-old. At the age of 23, he made his first-class debut for Middlesex, starting a brilliant career with the club which lasted nearly a decade and a half, playing in a County Championship-winning side four times and winning four one-day trophies with the club. 'Flash', as he was known to his teammates as a result of his ability to hurl the ball down at nearly 100 mph, picked up 532 first-class wickets for Middlesex at an average of 22.57 between the years of 1980 and 1993. Cowans went on to collect 19 Test caps for England, in which he took 51 wickets at an average of 39.27.

SATURDAY 18th APRIL 1998

One of the most successful Australian cricketers of his generation, Justin Lee Langer made his first-class debut for Middlesex in a four-day County Championship match against Kent at the St Lawrence Ground, Canterbury. Langer made 44 in Middlesex's first innings and 12 not out in their second, as Kent won a rain-affected match by four wickets. He joined Middlesex as their overseas player at the start of the 1998 season, and in 15 matches that season scored 1,448 runs for the club at an average of 62.95, including a highest score of 233 not out against Somerset at Lord's. Langer captained Middlesex in the 2000 season.

THURSDAY 19th APRIL 2007

In a match where records tumbled at the County Ground, Taunton, Somerset cruised to the highest-innings total ever scored against Middlesex in a first-class match, when they scored a phenomenal 850 for seven declared, which included a triple century (315) from ex Middlesex player and captain, Justin Langer, and hundreds from James Hildreth (116), Cameron White (114) and Peter Trego (130). This was only the second time in the club's history that four batsmen had scored hundreds in the same innings against Middlesex. Middlesex were not to be outdone however and achieved a draw in the game, thanks to scoring 600 for four declared themselves, the highest score they had ever posted in a first-class match against Somerset, with hundreds from Owais Shah (193), Billy Godleman (113*) and David Nash (100*).

SUNDAY 20th APRIL 2008

Andrew Strauss recorded his highest ever List-A career score, hitting 167 runs against Surrey at the Brit Oval in Middlesex's opening Friends Provident Trophy fixture of the 2008 season. Strauss faced 130 balls and batted for 145 minutes to compile his record innings, which included an incredible 23 fours and four sixes. Middlesex went on to post a total of 315 in their 50 overs, winning the match comfortably when they dismissed Surrey for just 248 in 43 overs, with Danny Evans taking three for 36 and Gareth Berg taking four for 50.

FRIDAY 21st APRIL 2006

When you're the grandson of Denis Compton, arguably one of the most famous cricketers to ever play for the club, you've already got a lot of pressure heaped upon you to live up to the astronomical standards set by your elder relative. Little wonder, therefore, that Nicholas Richard Denis (Nick) Compton breathed a huge sigh of relief when he made his maiden first-class hundred (101) for Middlesex, in a four-day game against the Oxford University Centre of Cricketing Excellence at the University Parks Ground in Oxford. While still scoring an impressive eight hundreds for Middlesex and nearly 3,000 first-class runs, Compton junior fell someway short of his grandfather's achievements, who scored an incredible 67 hundreds for the club in his brilliant career.

SATURDAY 22nd APRIL 1978

A Middlesex side, including legendary West Indies paceman Wayne Wendell Daniel and an array of other international Middlesex players, arrived at the Ransomes and Reavell Sports Club Ground in Ipswich to take on a Minor Counties East side in a Benson and Hedges Cup group match. The match proved to be the complete mismatch it had looked on paper, as Daniel wasted no time in ripping through the home side's batting line-up on his way to a record-breaking bowling performance. He finished with figures of seven for 12 from his 11 overs – the best ever List-A bowling figures recorded by a Middlesex player. The Minor Counties East side were dismissed for just 80, and Middlesex knocked off the runs within 32 overs to secure a comfortable eight-wicket victory.

THURSDAY 23rd APRIL 2009

Making his debut for Middlesex, Australia's latest young batting protégé Phillip Joel Hughes strode to the crease with a big reputation and a lot to prove for his new club. He left the Lord's pitch at the end of the day to a standing ovation, with an unbeaten hundred to his name. It was the first of his five centuries that he went on to score for Middlesex in just three first-class matches, leaving the club after just six weeks with a batting average of 143.50 and a highest score of 195 to his name. In Hughes' debut, against Glamorgan at Lord's, he scored 118 in Middlesex's first innings and followed this with 65 not out in their second, yet Middlesex could only draw their opening County Championship match of the season.

SUNDAY 24th APRIL 1994

Middlesex's reward for winning the County Championship in 1993 was to kick off the 1994 season with the Champion County match, a four-day affair against an England A side, packed full of existing and potential England internationals. Winning the toss and electing to field, only Kevin Shine shone with the ball for Middlesex, taking four for 79 as England A posted a total of 357 in their first innings. In reply, the Middlesex first innings collapsed, scoring just 156 when their final wicket fell. England A, with a point to prove and a 201-run first-innings lead, forced Middlesex to follow on. Middlesex had their captain and vice captain to thank for a second-innings total of 394 for four declared. Mike Gatting hit a quite brilliant 224 not out and John Carr an equally important 102 as Middlesex batted for 125 overs to save the game and start the new season with a creditable draw.

FRIDAY 25th APRIL 2008

In a County Championship match against Glamorgan at Lord's, Tim Murtagh recorded his best first-class bowling figures to date, taking seven for 95 in Glamorgan's first innings as the visitors were bowled out for 300 in reply to Middlesex's first-innings total of 308. Murtagh's seven wickets were not enough to secure victory, however, as the game finished in a draw.

FRIDAY 25th APRIL 1930

Middlesex cricketer Joseph Harold Anthony Hulme, who made 223 first-class appearances for the club between 1929 and 1939, had a day to remember. Aside from being a regular in Middlesex's ranks, he also played football for Herbert Chapman's Arsenal FC, and on this day he played outside right in the first of five FA Cup Final appearances he made. Arsenal won the match 2-0 in front of 92,499 fans at Wembley Stadium. In his Middlesex career he made 1,000 first-class runs in two separate seasons, 1932 and 1934, and scored a total of 8,015 runs for the club at an average of 26.62. For Arsenal he reached the FA Cup Final in 1927, 1930, 1932 and 1936, and won the First Division in the 1931, 1933, 1934 and 1935 seasons. He also reached the FA Cup Final for the fifth time with Huddersfield in 1938.

FRIDAY 26th APRIL 1895

Cyril Douglas Gray, who played for Middlesex between the years of 1925 and 1927, was born on this day in 1895, in Hampstead, North London. Gray played in just 15 first-class matches for Middlesex, but was lucky enough to have benefitted from playing in the same era as the great batsman Patsy Hendren. Gray scored 563 runs for Middlesex at an average of 23.45, but it was for an innings he played in a partnership with Hendren that he is best remembered. In less than two hours the pair of them put on an outstanding partnership of 214 runs at Lord's against Warwickshire in July 1927, despatching the ball with ease to all parts of the ground, with Gray himself scoring 81 runs and Hendren 156.

THURSDAY 27th APRIL 1995

John Donald Carr became only the second Middlesex player in the history of the club to take six catches as an outfield player in an opponent's innings. Four of his catches were taken off the bowling of off-spinner John Emburey, with the other two coming off the bowling of Phil Tufnell and Dion Nash. Despite Carr's safe hands in the field, Middlesex lost the County Championship match at Edgbaston to Warwickshire by 215 runs.

TUESDAY 28th APRIL 1942

John Michael (Mike) Brearley, one of the finest exponents of captaincy the game has ever seen, was born in Harrow, Middlesex. Brearley captained Middlesex between 1971 and 1982 and led the club to four separate County Championship victories in this time. He also captained England in 31 Test matches, losing just 4 of them. Along with Brearley's unerring understanding and ability to read a game, his record with the bat was equally impressive, as in his Middlesex career he scored 15,985 runs for the club at an average of 38.33. This aside, it was his ability to captain the side with such brilliance that has made him a true Middlesex legend.

MONDAY 29th APRIL 1966

One of the real characters in Middlesex's history, Philip Clive Roderick (Phil) Tufnell, was born in Barnet, Hertfordshire. Phil 'The Cat' Tufnell, a nickname he acquired from his fondness of napping in the Lord's dressing room, was considered by many to be a figure of fun. Often seen with a cigarette hanging from his mouth, Tufnell's relaxed and laidback approach to the game belied his abilities as a truly exceptional and often inspired left-arm orthodox spin bowler. In a Middlesex career spanning 16 years, between 1986 and 2002, Tufnell became the 13th-highest wicket taker in the club's history, taking 842 first-class wickets at an average of 28.16, with best bowling figures of eight for 29. Tufnell received 42 Test caps for England, taking 121 wickets at 37.68, with best bowling figures of seven for 47.

THURSDAY 30th APRIL 1987

At a Middlesex committee meeting, held at Lord's Cricket Ground, it was proposed that Denis Charles Scott Compton, at the age of 69, should be elected a life vice-president of the club, in honour of the years of dedicated service he gave to Middlesex County Cricket Club. Not surprisingly, the proposal received a unanimous vote in favour from all present at the meeting, who also proposed and agreed that a charity dinner in aid of the Centenary Youth Trust be held the following May at the Intercontinental Hotel in London to celebrate Compton's 70th birthday. After then standing and being voted in as Middlesex's President in 1991, Compton went on to serve in the role until 1997.

MIDDLESEX CCC
On This Day

MAY

WEDNESDAY 1st MAY 1968

While touring the West Indies with the England Test side in the winter of 1967/68, Frederick John (Fred) Titmus was the victim of a horrific boating accident in Barbados which saw him lose four toes on one foot. Many questioned whether this would end his brilliant career, but just a few months later, after a period of intensive recovery from his injury, he returned to fitness and was in the side playing for Middlesex in the season's opening County Championship fixture against Derbyshire at the County Ground. Any doubts over what effect the injury would have on Titmus's abilities to perform for Middlesex were soon dispelled, as he took an amazing 111 wickets that season at an average of just 19.37.

SATURDAY 2nd MAY 1992

The club record in List-A matches for a fifth wicket partnership was set by Mark Ravin Ramprakash and John Donald Carr in a Benson and Hedges Cup group match against Leicestershire at Grace Road, Leicester. Ramprakash's fine innings of 108 not out, and Carr's knock of 70, built a partnership of 147 and took the Middlesex score from 172 for four to 319 for five to set up a match-winning total for Middlesex of 325 from their allotted 55 overs. Leicestershire in reply could only make 226 for eight, and Middlesex won the match by 99 runs.

FRIDAY 3rd MAY 1867

The club's second-highest wicket taker of all time, John Thomas (Jack) Hearne, was born in Chalfont St Giles, Buckinghamshire. Hearne's Middlesex career spanned the years 1888 to 1923, during which he took an incredible 2,093 first-class wickets at an average of just 18.23, with career-best bowling figures of 9-23. He took five wickets in an innings on 171 separate occasions and ten wickets in a first-class match in 39 matches for the club. He had an incredible run of wicket-taking success for Middlesex, starting in 1891, when he took more than one hundred first-class wickets in a season for the first time, taking 118 wickets. He repeated the feat, taking more than 100 wickets in each of the next seven seasons for the club, with the 145 he took in 1893 being his most successful year.

TUESDAY 3rd MAY 1988

Angus Fraser became only the second player in Middlesex's history to take a hat-trick in a List-A match for the club. At Lord's against Sussex in a Benson and Hedges Cup group match, Fraser clean bowled the great Imran Khan, had Simon Kimber caught by Neil Williams and clean bowled Rodney Bunting. Fraser finished with figures of three for 39 from 11 overs in the match as Sussex made 182 for nine. Half centuries from Mike Gatting (56*) and John Carr (62) helped Middlesex to a five-wicket victory.

SUNDAY 4th MAY 1997

Playing an AXA Life League match against Essex at the County Ground in Chelmsford, Angus Fraser scored the highest ever List-A score by a Middlesex number 11 batsman in the club's history. Fraser had reached 33 runs before he was caught by Stuart Law off the bowling of Darren Robinson, but his record-breaking innings wasn't enough for Middlesex to avoid defeat, as they were bowled out for 190 chasing Essex's total of 256.

WEDNESDAY 4th MAY 2005

Playing against Northumberland in a Cheltenham and Gloucester Trophy match at Osborne Avenue, Jesmond, Middlesex batsmen Paul Weekes and Ed Smith set a new record for the highest ever opening partnership for Middlesex in List-A cricket. Having scored 206 in their innings, the last thing Northumberland needed was a solid opening stand from the Middlesex first pair. Just 31.3 overs later, Smith and Weekes had surpassed the Northumberland total to secure a ten-wicket victory for Middlesex. Weekes finished the innings unbeaten on 106, whilst Smith finished unbeaten on 96.

SUNDAY 5th MAY 2002

In a southern group match of the Benson and Hedges Cup in 2002, Australian Ashley Noffke scored the highest ever individual total by a number nine batsman for Middlesex in List-A cricket, scoring 58 runs from just 56 balls against Sussex at Lord's. Noffke's late cameo innings included three fours and one six, but wasn't enough to avoid a Middlesex defeat as they could only reach 224 in reply to Sussex's 252, and the south coast side won by 28 runs.

WEDNESDAY 5th MAY 2004

Middlesex's largest ever margin of victory in a List-A match came when playing against Wales Minor Counties in the C&G Trophy second round, at Lamphey Cricket Club Ground. Batting first, Middlesex posted a total of 277 for six in their 50 overs, with Jamie Dalrymple top-scoring with 104*. Middlesex then dismissed Wales MC for just 103, with Melvyn Betts taking four for 15. The margin of victory for Middlesex of 174 runs set a new club record. Dalrymple's innings of 104* still remains a club record for the highest ever List-A score by a Middlesex player batting at number six.

SUNDAY 6th MAY 2007

The Middlesex club record for the narrowest margin of wickets victory in a List-A match is just one wicket, with Middlesex winning twice by this margin. The latest of these was in a Friends Provident Trophy encounter with Gloucestershire at Lord's in a thrilling game. Having been set a target of 222 for victory, Middlesex seemed to be on course for a comfortable win, having reached 207 for five, just 15 short of victory. The falling of the sixth Middlesex wicket, that of Eoin Morgan, signalled a batting collapse of epic proportions, as Middlesex lost their next four wickets for just two runs. Number 11, Chris Wright, came to the crease to join number nine, Tim Murtagh, with the score on 209 for nine, needing another 13 runs for victory. Murtagh's 10* and Wright's 4* saw Middlesex over the line, securing a single wicket win for only the second time in their history in List-A cricket.

SUNDAY 7th MAY 1972

At the County Ground, Northampton, Middlesex won a bizarre John Player League encounter with Northamptonshire, when the home side set a new Club record for the lowest team total ever scored in a List-A match against Middlesex. The Northamptonshire side were in high spirits, feeling that they had the game won after dismissing Middlesex for a paltry 76 runs in just 29.2 overs. That was until they batted, as Middlesex dismissed them for a mere 41 runs in 32 overs to give Middlesex an unlikely 35-run win. Jim Stewart top-scored in the Northamptonshire innings with 12, but no other Northants batsman made double figures.

TUESDAY 7th MAY 1996

Glamorgan's Matthew Maynard made light work of the record books, when he scored 151 not out at Lord's in the Benson and Hedges Cup, as his innings was the highest ever score by an opposition number four batsman against Middlesex in List-A cricket. Glamorgan chased down Middlesex's target of 263 with seven balls to spare and six wickets in hand. Jason Pooley had earlier top-scored with 50 in the Middlesex innings.

SATURDAY 8th MAY 1937

One of Middlesex's most iconic players, William John (Bill) Edrich, made his first-class debut for Middlesex in a relatively non-eventful drawn County Championship fixture against Northamptonshire at Lord's. Edrich had to wait for the second day of the match before opening the batting with Reginald Butterworth, and made just 12 on his debut for the club, as he was out caught by Charles Davis off the bowling of medium pacer John Buswell. Edrich did however go on to make three first-class centuries for Middlesex in his debut season and got his highest score of the year, 175, against Lancashire at Lord's less than a month after making his debut. Edrich scored 2,154 runs in first-class cricket in his Middlesex debut season, playing also for MCC, for the South versus the North at Lord's and for an England XI against New Zealand.

SATURDAY 9th MAY 1981

Australian pace legend Jeff (Thommo) Thompson recorded the second-best List-A bowling figures in the club's history when taking seven for 22 in a thrilling Benson and Hedges Cup match against Hampshire at Lord's in 1981. Middlesex batted first and were bowled out for 175, with Clive Radley top-scoring with 50. Thompson opened the bowling for Middlesex and took three wickets to put Hampshire in deep trouble at 38 for four, before David Turner and John Rice put on 76 for the fifth wicket to put Hampshire back in the chase. In Thompson's second spell he then picked up another four wickets and Hampshire were seven down and struggling. It was left to Hampshire's number ten, Stephenson, and their number 11, Malone, to help them creep over the winning line with just three balls to spare to record a one-wicket win, and Thompson, despite his brilliant bowling performance, finished on the losing side.

SUNDAY 9th MAY 1982

In a John Player League fixture at the Phoenix County Ground in Bristol, Middlesex's Clive Radley scored the highest ever total by a Middlesex player batting at number five in List-A cricket, scoring 107* against Gloucestershire. Radley's innings came in a Middlesex total of 184, which was enough to secure a 20-run victory, as Gloucestershire were bowled out for just 164.

THURSDAY 10th MAY 1962

Middlesex's all-time leading wicket taker, Fred Titmus, took nine opposition wickets for Middlesex for the first time in his career in a match against Cambridge University at Fenner's. Titmus took nine for 52 from 32 overs as the university were bowled out for 121 in their second innings. Middlesex won the match by 225 runs.

TUESDAY 10th MAY 1977

In a nail-biting, rain-reduced 10-over Benson and Hedges Cup encounter at Lord's against Essex, Middlesex bowler Allan Arthur Jones became the first ever player in the club's history to take a List-A hat-trick. First he clean bowled Essex opener Ken McEwan for three, before dismissing incoming batsman Stewart Turner for a first ball duck, caught by Barlow. Essex captain Keith Fletcher faced the hat-trick ball, which he sent straight to Mike Smith, and Jones had his hat-trick. He went on to take five for 24 in the Essex innings, which reached just 60 for 8. Middlesex also reached 60, but won the match by virtue of having lost just two wickets.

MONDAY 11th MAY 2009

When playing against Kent at Canterbury in a Friends Provident Trophy match, Eoin Morgan posted the highest ever List-A total by a Middlesex player batting at number four, scoring 161 off just 136 balls. Morgan's innings included 19 fours and two sixes, as Middlesex posted 322 for five, the club's fifth-highest List-A-innings total ever. This was enough to see Middlesex to a convincing 80-run victory, as Kent were dismissed for 242. Morgan's innings also played a part in setting a new List-A record for the highest ever fourth wicket partnership for Middlesex as he put on 220 runs with Nick Compton. Compton's 131 was also his highest ever List-A score for Middlesex.

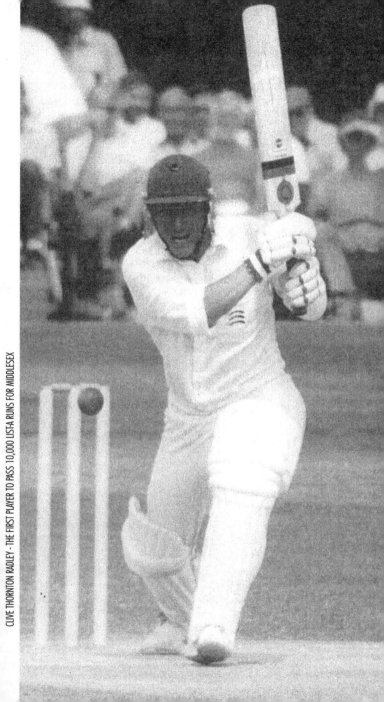

TUESDAY 12th MAY 2009

No Middlesex wicketkeeper in the club's history has ever claimed seven victims in a List-A fixture, but Warwickshire's Timothy Raymond (Tim) Ambrose did achieve the feat against Middlesex in a Friends Provident Trophy fixture at Edgbaston, claiming seven Middlesex batsmen's wickets with five catches and two stumpings. Middlesex were dismissed for 165 in a match that the home side won by six wickets.

SATURDAY 13th MAY 1978

In a Benson and Hedges Cup match at the County Ground in Hove, Wayne Daniel recorded the sixth-best List-A bowling figures ever by a Middlesex player when he took six for 17 as Sussex were bowled out for just 61 runs. Not surprisingly, Middlesex won the match by eight wickets, knocking off the runs with ease in only 8.1 overs for the loss of just two wickets.

WEDNESDAY 13th MAY 1903

James Morton (Jim) Sims, one of the most successful bowlers in Middlesex's early history, was born in Leyton, Essex. Sims, an unerringly accurate right-arm off-break bowler, played in 381 first-class matches for Middlesex and took an incredible 1,257 wickets for the club at an average of just 25.22. Sims' finest first-class spell for the club came against Lancashire at Old Trafford in August of 1934 in a County Championship match when he took 9-92 in the Lancashire innings. He took all ten wickets in an innings once (10 for 90), when playing in the East v West match. Sims' wicket tally makes him the fourth-highest first-class wicket taker of all time for the club.

SATURDAY 13th MAY 1944

Legendary Middlesex batsman and the fifth highest scorer of first-class runs in the club's history, Clive Thornton Radley, was born in Hertford. Radley is one of only nine batsmen to score more than 20,000 runs for the club, scoring 24,147 runs at an average of 35.45, including 42 centuries, in a Middlesex career spanning 1965 to 1987. Radley's finest season for Middlesex came in 1980, when he compiled 1,491 runs at an average of 57.34.

TUESDAY 14th MAY 1985

Middlesex had their captain, Mike Gatting, to thank for a Benson and Hedges Cup win over Sussex at the County Ground in Hove, as his innings of 143 not out set Middlesex up for a match-winning total of 280 for 5 in their 55 overs. Gatting's innings was the sixth highest individual innings by a Middlesex batsman in the club's List-A history, and was enough to secure Middlesex a 31-run victory, with Sussex managing to reach just 249 in reply before being bowled out.

TUESDAY 14th MAY 1996

Middlesex's Benson and Hedges Cup match against British Universities, played at the Fenner's Ground in Cambridge, set a new club record for the amount of extras that Middlesex have prospered from in any List-A match in their history. When British Universities batted and set Middlesex a moderate target of 185 to win, what they really needed was tight bowling and economic spells from their bowlers. What they dished up however was a barrage of wayward no-balls and wide deliveries, which must have caused the scorers no end of trouble. Not surprisingly, Middlesex won the game comfortably, although this was thanks largely to the extras column, which amassed an incredible 45 runs, including 24 no-balls and 19 wides, plus two leg byes. Extras finished as the game's second-highest scorer for Middlesex and were only surpassed by Paul Weekes, who scored 52.

SUNDAY 15th MAY 2005

Hampshire became the first side in history to score a total of 350+ against Middlesex in a List-A match, when they smashed a huge 353 for eight declared at Lord's. Paul Weekes was Middlesex's most economical bowler on the day, even though he went for a rather expensive 6.43 an over. In a Hampshire side packed with international talent, Australian Simon Katich top-scored for the visitors with 85 off just 63 balls, whilst Kevin Pietersen smashed 80 off just 50 balls. Middlesex never came close to chasing down the huge total, as Shaun Udal, who was to join Middlesex later in his career, took four for 55 with his off spin, as Middlesex were dismissed for 248 to lose the match by 105 runs.

SATURDAY 16th MAY 1959

A thrilling first-class encounter at Lord's saw Middlesex secure a win against Sussex by just one run. Being dismissed for just 220 in their first innings, Middlesex bounced back and rolled Sussex over for just 130, thanks largely to figures of seven for 54 from Fred Titmus. The Middlesex second innings showed no signs of batting getting any easier, as Sussex proceeded to bowl the home side out for just 138. With Sussex needing just 229 for victory, they looked to be home and dry at 209 for five, but a late collapse and a fine bowling spell on the final day by Middlesex's Alan Moss (5-42) saw the visitors bowled out for 227 and Middlesex winning the match by the tightest of margins.

SUNDAY 17th MAY 2009

Middlesex posted their highest ever List-A total, 341 for seven, in a 50-over match against Somerset at Lord's. Batting first, Middlesex had Australian Phillip Joel Hughes to largely thank for their total, as he scored a run-a-ball 112 for the home side. Amazingly, despite this being Middlesex's highest ever one-day total, Somerset went on to chase down their Duckworth Lewis rain adjusted target of 293 in just 39.1 overs, for the loss of only five wickets to secure a surprising victory.

MONDAY 18th MAY 2009

Middlesex went into their final Friends Provident Trophy group match of the 2009 season knowing that only a win against Warwickshire at Lord's would give them any chance of reaching the quarter finals of the tournament. Despite Warwickshire posting a hefty 276 for seven in their 50 overs, Middlesex chased down the required target for the loss of six wickets in a nail-biting last over of the match. Middlesex number six Neil Dexter (69 not out) and number eight Ben Scott (28 not out) were there at the end to score the winning runs for Middlesex. Scotland's unlikely victory over Kent, followed by a tied final Group B match of the campaign between Warwickshire and Kent left Middlesex in second place. The club fortuitously qualified for a knockout place in the quarter-finals, losing to Hampshire at the Rose Bowl.

WEDNESDAY 19th MAY 1948

One of the greatest and most widely talked about batting partnerships ever was fittingly completed by two of Middlesex's most legendary batsmen. Bill Edrich and Denis Compton compiled an unbelievable unbeaten partnership of 424 in a County Championship encounter with Somerset at Lord's. Edrich hit 168 not out and Compton scored 252 not out, which still remains the highest third wicket partnership in Middlesex's first-class history and the biggest batting partnership of all time for the club in any position. The achievement came in a Middlesex first-innings total of 478 for two declared, to which Somerset could only manage 194 all out in reply. Middlesex duly enforced the follow-on, and Somerset fared slightly better, posting 310 before being dismissed. Jack Robertson and Leslie Compton, Denis's brother, took no time at all in knocking off the winning 29 runs to secure a ten-wicket victory for Middlesex.

SATURDAY 20th MAY 1871

With Middlesex leading a somewhat nomadic existence at this time in their history, they found themselves with a 'home' ground at the Amateur Athletic Club at Lillie Bridge. The match that ended on this day was their one and only fixture to be played on the ground though, after they had moved on from their first home ground in Islington. Surrey were the opponents in a drawn match that was largely remembered for a fine innings by Middlesex middle-order batsman Bernard Pauncefote, who scored 94 not out. This was to be one of only three fixtures played by Middlesex in the entire 1871 season.

THURSDAY 20th MAY 2004

In a County Championship encounter between Middlesex and Surrey, Middlesex batsman Jamie Dalrymple posted a club record first-class score for a batsman batting at number six for Middlesex, completing an individual innings of 244 in a Middlesex total of 487 for nine declared. Dalrymple's innings came off 388 balls and included 38 boundaries. Dalrymple also broke another record with his massive innings, as it was the highest individual first-class innings of his career for Middlesex. Having scored 359 in their first innings, Surrey trailed Middlesex by 128 runs. They scored 300 for four in their second innings to earn a draw in the match.

MONDAY 21st MAY 1827

Long before the formation of the county club, there is on record a single wicket match that is well worthy of mention, held on Harefield Common, where "two gentlemen of Middlesex" competed against a local farmer from the Harefield area by the name of Frances Trumper. According to the records, Trumper was allowed to "have the help of his dog", which in hindsight was the downfall of the Middlesex gents. Trumper won the match by two wickets, although this is reported to be largely as a result of the adept fielding skills of his dog, who would sit to heel whilst the farmer delivered the ball. As soon as the ball was hit, the dog would fetch the ball back with such haste that the two gentlemen of Middlesex struggled to make any runs unless the ball was hit a huge distance.

SUNDAY 21st MAY 1899

Probably one of the shortest first-class County Championship encounters that Middlesex have ever taken part in started on this day, on what was scheduled to be a three-day match, yet which actually was concluded inside three hours. The first day's play, a bank holiday, was entirely lost due to persistent heavy rain, turning the wicket into a sodden mess which would today have been deemed unplayable. Unperturbed however, on the morning of day two the Somerset openers took their places at the crease, and just 15 overs later they and the entire Somerset batting line-up were dismissed for a meagre first-innings total of 35. Middlesex's batsmen faired only slightly better, finishing on 86 all out from just 38.2 overs. Trailing by 51, Somerset's second-innings totalled only 44 in just 16.3 overs, and they lost the match by an innings and 7 runs, ending in less than one day. Middlesex bowlers JT Hearne and AE Trott finished with match figures of eight for 44 and 11 for 31 respectively.

SATURDAY 21st MAY 1977

In a Benson and Hedges Cup match against Northamptonshire at the County Ground in Northampton, Graham Barlow scored the second-highest ever List-A score of his career for Middlesex with 129 runs in a Middlesex total of 303. Northamptonshire were then bowled out for 224 and Middlesex won by 79 runs.

WEDNESDAY 22nd MAY 1907

One of the finest individual bowling performances by a Middlesex bowler is undoubtedly that of Albert Edwin Trott who, in a County Championship match against Somerset at Lord's, took two hat-tricks in the same innings. With Somerset needing 264 to win in the fourth innings of the game, Trott's amazing feat started with the wicket of Somerset number four, Talbot Lewis, lbw for 1. Trott then clean bowled Massey Poyntz, Sammy Woods and Ernie Robson, all for first ball ducks, to claim four wickets in four balls. With Somerset reeling at 92 for seven, Trott wasn't done yet. In three successive balls, he then had Osbert Mordaunt caught behind for four, bowled Archie Wickham first ball and had Albert Bailey caught behind to dismiss Somerset for just 97. Trott finished with figures of seven for 20 in the innings, and Middlesex comfortably won the game by 166 runs. No other Middlesex bowler in history has repeated Trott's remarkable feat, which he achieved more than a century ago.

THURSDAY 23rd MAY 1918

One of the greatest Middlesex players of all time, Denis Charles Scott Compton, was born in Hendon, Middlesex. Compton became a true legend of Middlesex cricket in his time at the club, and the memories of his free-flowing run scoring will live on forever. In his Middlesex career, which spanned 1936 to 1958, Compton scored a massive 21,781 runs at an average of 49.95, including 67 centuries and a highest individual score of 263. Compton was a more than useful bowler too on his day, and as a slow left-arm Chinaman he picked up 477 first-class wickets for Middlesex at an average of 29.61.

SUNDAY 23rd MAY 2010

Playing against the Netherlands in Holland at Amstelveen, Middlesex's Scott Newman scored his highest ever List-A score for the club, as Newman's 122 runs helped Middlesex to a total of 241 in this Clydesdale Bank 40 group match. Newman's innings came off just 107 balls and included fourteen fours and three sixes. Middlesex then dismissed the Netherlands for 195 to secure a win by 46 runs.

WEDNESDAY 24th MAY 1950

When Bill Edrich led out the Middlesex side at Lord's against Derbyshire at the start of a four-day County Championship match, he was the second captain to take charge of the side already this season, following on from Robert Walter Vivian (Walter) Robins, who captained the side in the season's opening games. Edrich led Middlesex to a draw in the match versus Derbyshire, but little would he have known of the difficulties that lay ahead for the club throughout the 1950 season. Amazingly, Robins and Edrich were the first two of seven different captains that led out the Middlesex side in first-class matches this season, setting an unenviable record that is unlikely to ever be beaten. On that list with Bill Edrich and Walter Robins were some other great Middlesex legends in Denis Compton, Jim Sims, Gubby Allen, John Dewes and George Mann.

FRIDAY 24th MAY 2002

Middlesex's Sven Koenig scored his highest ever List-A score for Middlesex in a Cheltenham and Gloucester Trophy match at Chelmsford against Essex. Koenig opened the batting with Andrew Strauss and scored 116 runs at more than a run a ball, hitting nine fours and two sixes from the 115 balls he faced. Despite Koenig's highest ever innings, Middlesex could only post a total of 291, which never looked enough on an exceptional Chelmsford batting track. So it proved, as Essex took the gloss off Koenig's day by reaching their target with an over and a half to spare to record a five-wicket win.

MONDAY 25th MAY 1914

Middlesex batsman, Francis Alfred (Frank) Tarrant, scored the highest-ever first-class individual score for a Middlesex player batting at position number two. His record-breaking innings of 250 not out has remained intact for nearly a century, and came in an-innings total of 464 for one declared against Essex in a County Championship match at the County Ground, Leyton. Middlesex went on to bowl out Essex for 173 in their first innings and 235 in their second to secure a comfortable victory in the match by an innings and 56 runs.

SATURDAY 25th MAY 1968

The first Middlesex batsman to ever score a century in List-A cricket was opening batsman Eric Russell, scoring 123 against Surrey at Lord's in the Gillette Cup. Russell's innings was finally ended when he was run out, selflessly looking to push the score along. Middlesex scored 220 in their 60 overs, before dismissing Surrey for just 117 to secure a win by a margin of 103 runs.

SATURDAY 26th MAY 1906

In a County Championship match between Middlesex and Sussex at Lord's, Sussex opener Charles Fry collapsed in agony attempting a quick single off the bowling of JT Hearne, having torn the Achilles tendon in his left leg. Being no place for sympathy, none was shown, and the Sussex batsman was duly run out, and had to then be carried from the field of play in horrendous pain to the pavilion by the Middlesex fielders. Sussex never recovered and their second innings collapsed to just 120 all out, leaving Middlesex with the relatively simple task of scoring 112 to win the match – a task they achieved for the loss of six wickets.

MONDAY 27th MAY 1968

In a Gillette Cup match against Surrey at Lord's, John Thomas (JT) Murray became the first wicketkeeper in Middlesex's history to claim five victims in a List-A fixture. All five of his dismissals were caught behind, and his first two victims were legendary Surrey batsmen John Hugh Edrich, cousin of Middlesex's Bill, and Michael James (Micky) Stewart. Murray went on to claim five victims in List-A fixtures for Middlesex on two other occasions, both in 1975, against Essex and again against Surrey.

MONDAY 28th MAY 1883

Middlesex came up against the finest cricketer of his generation, WG Grace, on a day that the great 'WG' was on song with both bat and ball. Despite Middlesex winning the match by 85 runs, WG put on a one-man show of defiance to make it hard work for Middlesex, scoring 89 in Gloucestershire's first innings and 35 in their second. He rounded off a fine individual performance by also taking five Middlesex wickets for 64 in their first innings, and then seven for 92 in their second.

THURSDAY 29th MAY 1890

Making his debut for Middlesex at Lord's, and setting the scene for what was to become a truly brilliant career with Middlesex, was John Thomas (Young Jack) Hearne. The Middlesex side of this era had long missed a quality fast bowler, and in Hearne they found one. On his debut against a Nottinghamshire side, who went into the game as firm favourites, Hearne took apart the Notts first innings batting, taking 6 for 62, and then followed this up with 1 for 45 in the second innings. His endeavours secured Middlesex a surprising victory by seven wickets, and started Hearne on a Middlesex career path which would see him become the club's leading first-class wicket taker of all time for a pace bowler.

SATURDAY 29th MAY 2004

Middlesex's Jamie Dalrymple equalled the record for the highest ever individual score by a number five batsman for Middlesex in List-A cricket, when he scored 107 against Glamorgan at Lord's in a Cheltenham and Gloucester Trophy match. Dalrymple's innings came off just 108 balls and included 14 boundaries. He helped Middlesex to reach the Glamorgan target of 256, and Middlesex won the match by six wickets.

THURSDAY 30th MAY 1929

Middlesex batsman, John William (Young Jack) Hearne, started an innings that would see him post an incredible score of 285 not out, to record the highest ever score by a Middlesex batsman at number three in a first-class match. His huge score was completed on the final day of the County Championship match against Essex at the County Ground in Leyton, when Middlesex posted a first-innings total of 486 all out in a match that finished in a draw.

THURSDAY 31st MAY 1787

Thomas Lord, founder of Middlesex's modern day home ground, the current Lord's Cricket Ground in St John's Wood, played his first competitive fixture for Middlesex on his 'own' ground, now referred to as the 'Lord's Old Ground', which was situated in Dorset Square, Marylebone, London. The match, between Middlesex and Essex, saw Middlesex win by 93 runs, and Thomas Lord, given that he owned the ground, chose to open the batting in both Middlesex innings, scoring just one and 36.

MIDDLESEX CCC
On This Day

JUNE

SUNDAY 1st JUNE 1980

Middlesex captain Mike Brearley scored one of his three List-A centuries for Middlesex against Somerset in the John Player League match at Taunton. The Somerset side included Ian Botham and Sunil Gavaskar, but they were no match on the day for Brearley's men. Brearley scored 109 not out as Middlesex posted 241, Somerset were dismissed for just 119, and Middlesex won by 122 runs.

SATURDAY 1st JUNE 1991

Playing for Kent against Middlesex in a County Championship match at Lord's, visiting wicketkeeper Steve Marsh had a game that he will remember for a long time. He took an incredible eight catches behind the stumps as Middlesex were dismissed for just 163 runs in their first innings. In Middlesex's history, Marsh is the only wicketkeeper to claim more than six victims in a first-class innings against the club.

THURSDAY 2nd JUNE 1864

Although not classed as a first-class fixture, Middlesex embarked upon their opening post formation fixture, a game played at Bury Field, Newport Pagnell, with Buckinghamshire in opposition. The Middlesex side was captained by John Walker, and included him and three of his brothers from the famous Walker family of Southgate. One of them, Vyell, finished the match with 11 wickets to his name, whilst Bucks player Thomas Hearne took seven Middlesex first innings wickets and clearly impressed his opponents, as following this game he joined Middlesex. Middlesex's opening competitive fixture finished in a draw.

TUESDAY 2nd JUNE 1936

Denis Charles Scott Compton made his first-class debut against Sussex at Lord's as an 18-year-old in a match which ended in a draw. Coming into the side as the new boy, Compton was told to bat at number 11 and reached the crease to join Middlesex legend Gubby Allen at the other end, with Middlesex still needing 24 runs to achieve a first-innings lead. Compton showed plenty of what was to come as he dug in against Sussex's fiery paceman Maurice Tait, who already had six wickets to his name and fancied young Compton as his seventh, to put on a 36-run last wicket partnership with Allen to earn Middlesex a first-innings lead.

THURSDAY 3rd JUNE 2010

The 2010 Friends Provident Twenty20 season got underway with a home tie against Sussex and with a very new look and feel to Twenty20 cricket at Lord's. Pinky the Panther, the club's new mascot, made his debut appearance, as did the Pantherettes, Middlesex's brand new dance troupe. Three Middlesex fans had the opportunity to win a million Australian dollars on the pitch during the interval of the match – the new world of Twenty20 cricket had definitely reached Lord's. Sussex ran out winners in the match by 28 runs, although Middlesex fans did get to see the great Australian legend, Adam Gilchrist, making his debut and opening the batting for the Panthers.

MONDAY 4th JUNE 1877

Having reached an agreement with Marylebone Cricket Club to play at Lord's Cricket Ground, Middlesex's opening first-class match at what was to become their permanent home in St John's Wood for more than 130 years was against a strong visiting Yorkshire side. Batting first, the visitors were dismissed for 182 before Middlesex themselves took a first-innings lead, posting a total of 203. Yorkshire were then dismissed for 230, leaving Middlesex with a target of 210 runs for victory. Sadly the result didn't live up to the occasion, as Middlesex were bowled out for 174 to kick off things at their new home with a loss by a margin of 35 runs.

THURSDAY 4th JUNE 1963

Middlesex suffered their narrowest runs defeat in first-class history in their County Championship match against Sussex at Lord's, losing by just one run – a feat they repeated again in July of 1976. In reply to Sussex's first-innings total of 212, Middlesex posted 324 and took a first-innings lead of 112. Fred Titmus's six for 69 saw Sussex again dismissed cheaply in their second innings, for just 223, to leave Middlesex needing only 112 to secure a win on the third and final day of the match. Middlesex never recovered from a terrible start, collapsing to 110 all out to give Sussex a most unlikely victory.

FRIDAY 5th JUNE 1909

Amazingly, despite being the club's leading first-class run scorer of all time with more than 40,000 runs to his name, it took Elias Henry (Patsy) Hendren 16 innings to reach his first half century for Middlesex. Prior to getting his maiden half century, his record showed little of what was to come, as he had scored only 103 runs at an average of just 7.92, including a shocking seven ducks. His maiden half century came, as did no doubt a huge sigh of relief, in a County Championship game against Hampshire at Lord's ending on this day, when he scored 75 runs in a Middlesex total of 207.

MONDAY 5th JUNE 1911

Having taken 16 innings to reach his first half century for the club, staggeringly it took Middlesex's all-time leading first-class run scorer, Patsy Hendren, another two years for him to score his maiden first-class century. He achieved the feat when scoring 134 not out in a seven-wicket victory for Middlesex over Sussex at Lord's, which started on exactly the same day as the match in which he had scored his half century had ended two years earlier. Unbelievably, it had taken Hendren a shocking 57 first-class matches to reach the milestone of a maiden century, in which he had batted in 87 innings and was only averaging 19.55 until that point. Such patience from selectors in today's game would not be shown, but thankfully things were different in Hendren's era, as he went on to score more than 40,000 runs for the club.

THURSDAY 6th JUNE 1957

Michael William (Mike) Gatting, the second-highest first-class run scorer in Middlesex's history, was born in Kingsbury, Middlesex. Gatting, who made his debut for Middlesex in 1975, played for the club for 24 seasons and captained the side between 1983 and 1997 through some of the county's most successful years. In his Middlesex career he amassed an incredible total of 28,411 runs at an average of 52.80, scoring 77 hundreds in the process. Gatting was also held in high regard for his captaincy, leading Middlesex to success in the County Championship on three separate occasions in 1985, 1990 and 1993, and captained England to an Ashes series victory in the 1986/87 season.

TUESDAY 7th JUNE 1864

Middlesex completed their first ever first-class cricket match, a two-day encounter with Sussex which Middlesex won by an innings and 54 runs. It was a match to remember for Vyell Edward (VE) Walker, who took nine for 63 off 40 overs in the first innings as Sussex made just 111, and then followed it up with figures of five for 48 from 35 overs in the Sussex second innings as they were dismissed for just 98. Incredibly, Middlesex only used two bowlers in the entire match, with Walker bowling 75 overs, and Thomas Hearne bowling 77 from the other end.

WEDNESDAY 8th JUNE 1927

At the County Ground in Leyton, Middlesex batsman Patsy Hendren broke yet another Middlesex record. What made this one slightly surprising was that Jack Durston, a man known more for his bowling prowess than his batting, was also involved. Hendren and Durston put on an unbeaten partnership of 160 to record the highest ever ninth wicket partnership in the club's first-class history. Their record-breaking partnership set up a Middlesex total of 428 for eight declared, which they defended by bowling out Essex twice for 181 and 144 to secure an innings and 103 runs victory.

WEDNESDAY 9th JUNE 1937

Only one Middlesex wicketkeeper in history has claimed seven first-class victims in one innings. Wilfred Frederick Frank (Frank) Price achieved the feat in a County Championship match against Yorkshire at Lord's in a match that Middlesex won by an innings and 22 runs. All seven of Price's dismissals were caught behind, with four of them coming off the bowling of Jim Smith, who took six for 75.

WEDNESDAY 9th JUNE 1982

Wayne Daniel recorded his best ever first-class bowling figures for Middlesex in a County Championship match against Glamorgan at St Helen's, Swansea. Glamorgan were dismissed for 191, with Mike Gatting taking five for 34, before Middlesex made 352 in their first innings. Daniel then took career-best bowling figures of nine for 61 from 21.4 overs to bowl out Glamorgan for 202 in their second innings, leaving Middlesex needing just 42 to win, which they reached without loss.

SATURDAY 9th JUNE 1984

Mike Gatting, Middlesex's second-highest run scorer in history, posted his highest ever first-class-innings total for Middlesex, scoring a massive 258 against Somerset at the Recreation Ground in Bath. Gatting's innings surpassed his previous best ever of 216, and was part of a Middlesex first-innings total of 473 for 7 declared. The Middlesex total was only enough to earn Middlesex a draw however, as Somerset bounced back with a first-innings total of 516 themselves in reply.

MONDAY 10th JUNE 1867

So strong was the batting of Middlesex considered to be in this era that they were selected and invited by Marylebone Cricket Club to take on the England side of the day at Lord's Cricket Ground in the club's season-opening fixture. The challenge proved too much for Middlesex against a strong England side including both WG Grace and his brother Edward. Chasing England's first-innings total of 261, Middlesex were dismissed twice, for just 101 in their first innings, with WG Grace taking six for 53, and again for 135 in their second, with WG taking two for 35. England won the match convincingly by an innings and 25 runs.

TUESDAY 10th JUNE 1919

In a County Championship match against Hampshire at Lord's, Middlesex batsmen Patsy Hendren and Jack Hearne recorded the highest ever first-class fourth wicket partnership for Middlesex of 325 runs. In a match that Middlesex comprehensively won, by an innings and 74 runs, Hendren scored a magnificent 201, and Hearne remained unbeaten on 218 not out in a Middlesex total of 608 for seven declared.

FRIDAY 11th JUNE 2004

New Zealand batsman Craig Murray Spearman scored the highest ever individual first-class score against a Middlesex side in the County Championship, in a game played at Archdeacon Meadow, Gloucester. His score of 341 off 390 balls included 40 fours and six sixes in an innings that lasted 534 minutes. Gloucestershire went on to post a huge total of 695 in the match, seeing them on their way to securing a ten-wicket victory over Middlesex.

ELIAS HENRY 'PATSY' HENDREN – MIDDLESEX'S ALL TIME LEADING RUN SCORER

WEDNESDAY 11th JUNE 2008

When Texan oil billionaire Sir Allen Stanford landed his helicopter on the Nursery Ground at Lord's Cricket Ground to launch his Twenty20 for 20 Stanford Super Series, little did Middlesex know at the time that they would be competing for a share of the $20 million riches on offer in Antigua later that year as a result of winning the 2008 Twenty20 Cup. Stanford's brash arrival at Lord's, complete with a Sikorsky helicopter and an armoured car allegedly containing the $20 million, was widely criticised by many within the game as 'just not cricket'.

MONDAY 12th JUNE 1871

One of only three matches played by Middlesex in the season was at Lord's against Marylebone Cricket Club, which saw Middlesex batsman Walter Henry Hadow make history by becoming the first ever Middlesex player to score an individual double century in a first-class match. Hadow's innings lasted five and a half hours, was interrupted several times by rain, and included four fives and sixteen fours. Middlesex went on to beat MCC by an innings and 55 runs.

MONDAY 12th JUNE 1899

Rarely have innings from a number nine and number eleven batsman been as influential and rarely has an innings been rescued so brilliantly by its tail as they were in a match between Middlesex and Kent in the County Championship at Lord's. When Richard William Nicholls strode to the crease at number nine, with the Middlesex score only on 50 for eight, few would have banked upon Nicholls saving the game for Middlesex. That said, he proceeded to score the highest ever Middlesex first-class score for a number nine batsman, scoring a staggering 154. He was also very well assisted by a certain William Roche, who at number eleven came to the crease with the score on 55 for 9 and joined Nicholls. They proceeded to score the highest ever tenth wicket partnership for Middlesex, an amazing 230, which included 74 not out from Roche – the highest ever score in a first-class match for a Middlesex number 11. The Middlesex first-innings total surprisingly reached 285, which was enough to see them secure the most unlikely of victories by a margin of 118 runs.

WEDNESDAY 13th JUNE 1923

Middlesex started a three-day County Championship match against Hampshire at the County Ground, Southampton, where they posted the largest first-class score in the club's history, scoring 642 for three declared in their first innings. The innings included three figures scores from each of Middlesex's top four batsmen; Hugh Dales (103), Henry Lee (107), Jack Hearne (232) and Patsy Hendren (177). Despite this huge total, the match only ended in a draw.

SATURDAY 14th JUNE 1997

Glamorgan were dismissed by Middlesex for just 31, equalling the unenviable record set by Gloucestershire as the lowest ever first-class total scored in an innings against Middlesex. Only one Glamorgan batsman, Phillip Cottey, made it into double figures, with 12. Angus Fraser (four for 17) and James Hewitt (six for 14) were responsible for the damage, as Middlesex won the match inside three days.

SATURDAY 15th JUNE 1929

George Oswald Browning (Gubby) Allen made history in a first-class County Championship match against Lancashire at Lord's with a truly memorable bowling display that saw him become only the third bowler in Middlesex's history to take all ten opposition wickets in an innings and claim the record for the best ever bowling figures delivered by a Middlesex bowler. His memorable bowling performance came in Lancashire's first innings, when he bowled 25.3 overs, ten of which were maidens, taking ten wickets for just 40 runs as Lancashire were dismissed for 241. Allen can consider himself slightly unlucky that even this wasn't enough to win the game for Middlesex, which ended in a draw.

TUESDAY 15th JUNE 2010

Middlesex off spinner Tom Smith recorded the fourth-best ever bowling figures in a Twenty20 fixture by a Middlesex player when taking four for 23 against Glamorgan at Richmond. Middlesex had posted a huge total of 213, thanks mainly to 51 runs from Australia's Adam Gilchrist and 79 not out from England's Eoin Morgan. The Middlesex total was the club's highest ever total in a Twenty20 match. In reply, Smith's four wickets helped dismiss Glamorgan for just 129 runs, to see Middlesex secure a massive 84-run victory.

MONDAY 16th JUNE 1924

Not once in the club's history has an opposition bowler taken all ten Middlesex wickets in an innings in a first-class match. Somerset bowler Raymond Charles Robertson-Glasgow came the closest however and holds the record of having the finest first-class bowling figures against a Middlesex side. His right-arm fast-medium action accounted for nine of the Middlesex batsmen, when he took 9 for 38, with 9 maidens off 22.4 overs. His spell saw the Middlesex innings collapse to 128 all out, in reply to Somerset's 178. Somerset were then rolled over for just 136 leaving Middlesex needing 187 to win. Robertson-Glasgow then took another 3 for 81, as Middlesex were dismissed for 148 to give Somerset a 37-run victory.

WEDNESDAY 17th JUNE 1914

The final day of a County Championship match between Middlesex and Lancashire saw Lancashire cling on for a draw at Lord's, which was a fantastic result for them as they had been forced to follow on by Middlesex. Middlesex had both Frank Tarrant and Jack Hearne to thank for enabling them to enforce the follow-on, batting Middlesex towards a total of 501 for three declared and compiling the highest ever first-class partnership scored for the second wicket in Middlesex's history, 380 runs. Tarrant scored 198 and Hearne 204 before both lost their wickets in quick succession.

SATURDAY 18th JUNE 2005

An amazing County Championship match at The Walker Ground, Southgate, saw the highest ever match aggregate posted in a first-class Middlesex match. Batting first, Glamorgan posted a total of 584 for three declared, with hundreds from Cherry (226), Hemp (103) and Hughes (134*). In reply, Middlesex posted a total of 435 for four declared, with Ed Joyce scoring an unbeaten 155. Glamorgan declared in their second innings on 256 for three, with another hundred (100*) from Hughes, leaving Middlesex needing more than 400 in their fourth innings to secure an unlikely win. Thanks to hundreds from Ed Smith (145) and Owais Shah (155) and an unbeaten innings of 70 from Ed Joyce, Middlesex scored 408 for four to secure a six-wicket victory, with an unbelievable 1,683 runs being scored in the match.

FRIDAY 19th JUNE 1936

A special day for one of the greatest batsmen ever to play for Middlesex, as an 18-year-old Denis Charles Scott Compton made his maiden first-class century, 100 not out, in Middlesex's first innings of a County Championship match against Northamptonshire, just three weeks after making his debut for the side in the season's opening fixture against Sussex. Compton's hundred helped Middlesex to a total of 464 in reply to Northants' first innings of 298. Northants clung on and reached 141 for eight in their second innings to earn a draw. This was to be the first of 67 hundreds he scored for the club in his career.

SUNDAY 19th JUNE 1994

In an AXA Equity and Law match at Grace Road, Leicester, Leicestershire batsman and West Indies legend Phil Simmons scored the highest ever individual score by a number one batsman against Middlesex in List-A cricket, smashing his way to 140 runs as Leicestershire posted a huge total of 301 in their 40 overs. In reply, Middlesex always struggled before eventually being dismissed for 240, to lose the match by 61 runs. Mark Feltham top-scored for Middlesex with 75 runs at number seven.

SATURDAY 20th JUNE 1925

At the time, Middlesex had never chased a total of any more than 350 in the fourth innings of a match to win the game at any point in their history. When Nottinghamshire set them a target of 502 to win at Trent Bridge on the final day of this County Championship match, there weren't many that thought Middlesex would even get close. The task looked even more unlikely when Middlesex were reduced to 231 for six in their chase. Enter Frank Mann to join Patsy Hendren at the crease and commence their record-breaking antics. Their unbeaten partnership of 271 remains the highest ever seventh wicket partnership in the club's history, and it also took Middlesex to their target of 502 for an amazing and unlikely victory by four wickets, which to this day remains the highest ever fourth-innings total a Middlesex side have chased down to win a first-class game.

TUESDAY 21st JUNE 1870

After losing residency at the Cattle Market Ground in Islington in 1869 after many disputes with their landlord, Middlesex were technically homeless. Their efforts to rent the Amateur Athletics Ground at Lillie Bridge near West Brompton proved successful, but the ground was deemed unfit to play cricket on. Middlesex therefore only played two fixtures in the 1870 season, both away at the Kennington Oval. The first match saw Middlesex beat Surrey by four wickets, thanks largely again to one of the Walker brothers, with ID Walker scoring an unbeaten 94 to help Middlesex recover from 37 for three and take them to their target of 183 to win the game.

SUNDAY 22nd JUNE 2003

Not surprisingly, the club record that exists for the lowest margin that Middlesex have won a List-A match by is one run, which has occurred on 11 separate occasions. What is surprising, however, is that four of those one-run victories have come against unfortunate Nottinghamshire sides! The last of these was in a National League fixture at Trent Bridge, when Middlesex posted a total of 234. Chasing their target, Notts looked to be perfectly on course for the win, even when Kevin Pietersen fell for 82 off 70 balls with the score on 173 for four. The Notts innings then ground to a halt, as they stuttered along to 233 for eight at the close of their innings to suffer yet another defeat to Middlesex by the narrowest of margins.

WEDNESDAY 22nd JUNE 2005

When Middlesex beat Hampshire at the Rose Bowl in the Twenty20 Cup, they scored 200 runs in a Twenty20 innings for the first time in the club's history. A blistering innings of 72 runs from Owais Shah from just 32 balls faced, including eight fours and four sixes, got Middlesex off to a flying start and on their way to a new club record. Hampshire's New Zealander, Craig MacMillan, suffered most at the hands of Shah, being smashed for 28 runs from the single over he bowled, whilst James Bruce and Shaun Udal went for 13 and 12 an over respectively. Hampshire put up a good fight in reply, and fell just eight runs short on 192.

TUESDAY 23rd JUNE 1896

The first Middlesex player to have his name assigned to the famous Lord's honours board for an international bowling performance was John Thomas (Jack) Hearne, for taking five wickets for 76 for England against Australia on the second day of the opening Ashes Test at Lord's. England won the match by 66 runs and went on to claim a 2-1 series win under the leadership of WG Grace, with Hearne taking 15 wickets during the three Test matches.

SUNDAY 23rd JUNE 1974

In a 40-over John Player League match played at Headingley, Leeds, Middlesex were dismissed for their lowest ever List-A total, just 23 runs, by Yorkshire. Not surprisingly, no Middlesex batsman made double figures in the innings, and five were dismissed for ducks. Chasing Yorkshire's total of 148, the Middlesex innings was wrapped up in just 19.4 overs, with opener Clive Radley top-scoring for Middlesex with just six runs. The most expensive Yorkshire bowler was Arthur Robinson, who went for nine runs from his six overs, although he did take three wickets.

THURSDAY 23rd JUNE 2005

Middlesex's Owais Shah and Scott Styris put on 109 for the second wicket to record the highest ever second wicket partnership for Middlesex in Twenty20 cricket, against Surrey at Lord's. Chasing a target of 201 for victory, things were seemingly going well until Shah fell for 78 and Styris for 40. Middlesex had reached 160 for four when the mother of all collapses happened, as Middlesex lost their last six wickets for just 17 runs, without a single batsman after Styris, at number three, getting into double figures.

WEDNESDAY 24th JUNE 1987

Playing at Feethams Cricket Ground, Darlington, in a NatWest Trophy fixture against Durham, Middlesex's Clive Thornton Radley became the first player in the club's history to pass 10,000 List-A runs in a career. He achieved the feat in a relatively innocuous innings of 28 in a Middlesex total of 155 for three, which was enough to see Middlesex to a seven-wicket win, chasing down the Durham total of 151 inside 52 overs.

WEDNESDAY 24th JUNE 1992

Middlesex openers Desmond Haynes and Mike Roseberry kicked off a NatWest Bank Trophy match against lowly Shropshire at Telford with a huge opening partnership of 199. The Shropshire bowlers offered little with the new ball, as Roseberry smashed his way to 112 and Haynes scored a majestic 101. When the Shropshire opening bowler, Giles Toogood, returned for a second spell he had got the ball swinging and lived up to his name with a spell that was 'too good'. He took six for 47 and Middlesex reached 294 in their innings. Shropshire were then dismissed for just 149 and Middlesex won by 145 runs.

WEDNESDAY 24th JUNE 1998

Playing in a NatWest Bank Trophy match at Lord's against Herefordshire, Australian opening batsman Justin Langer scored his highest ever List-A score for Middlesex when he smashed 114 not out. Langer's innings was in a Middlesex total of 215, which they scored to win the match, chasing down Herefordshire's total of 213. Langer's innings came off 136 balls and included 13 fours.

TUESDAY 24th JUNE 2008

Dawid Malan and Eoin Morgan played their part in a Middlesex Twenty20 victory over Kent at Uxbridge Cricket Club, posting the record fourth wicket partnership in Twenty20 cricket for Middlesex, scoring 94 runs. Morgan finished with 62 runs from just 43 balls, including five huge sixes and three fours, and Malan hit 52 not out from 34 balls, picking up three sixes and three fours. Middlesex posted a total of 171 for seven in their 20 overs before restricting Kent to just 165.

THURSDAY 24th JUNE 2010

Middlesex off spinner Tom Smith became only the second person in the club's history to take five wickets in a Twenty20 match when he claimed five for 24 at Lord's against the Kent Spitfires. Smith's efforts helped dismiss Kent for 141, 13 runs short of their target, and Middlesex won the match. Smith joined Middlesex from Sussex at the start of the 2010 season and claimed 18 Twenty20 wickets in his first season with the club, at an average of just 17.27.

WEDNESDAY 25th JUNE 1913

Middlesex had their tail to thank for setting up an innings and 85 runs victory over Nottinghamshire at Lord's, as at 256 for seven Harry Robert (Joe) Murrell came to the crease at number nine to join number eight, Mordaunt Henry Caspers Doll. They proceeded to put on the highest eighth-wicket partnership in the club's history, an incredible unbeaten 182, of which Doll got 102 not out and Murrell got 71 not out to see the Middlesex total to 438 for seven declared. Middlesex then dismissed Nottinghamshire for 144 and 209 to secure an unlikely innings victory.

FRIDAY 26th JUNE 1868

In possibly one of the strangest ever innings for Middlesex, in a County match against Kent at the Bat and Ball ground in Gravesend, Middlesex opening batsman Thomas Hearne became one of only two batsmen in the history of the club to open the batting for Middlesex and carry his bat through an all-out innings, to finish on 0*. Middlesex lost the game, so whatever his game plan was it evidently didn't work. Hearne dead-batted his way through the entire innings of 61 overs to claim this bizarre record.

SUNDAY 26th JUNE 1988

Playing for Middlesex in a Refuge Assurance League match at Lord's in 1988, Keith Robert Brown, batting at number seven, scored the highest ever individual-innings total by a batsman in that position in List-A cricket for Middlesex. His innings of 102 wasn't enough to avoid a defeat in the game for Middlesex, as they fell 27 runs short of chasing down Somerset's total of 247.

TUESDAY 27th JUNE 1995

Middlesex owed a victory over lowly Cornwall in the NatWest Bank Trophy to opening batsman Paul Weekes, as his 143 not out proved essential in Middlesex overcoming the cricketing minnows. Weekes's innings equalled the seventh-highest total by any Middlesex batsman in List-A cricket, and it helped Middlesex reach 304 in their 60 overs, with 30 being the next-highest score for Middlesex. In reply, Cornwall struggled and only reached 200 in their innings, but without Weekes's innings things could have easily worked out differently.

SATURDAY 27th JUNE 1998

At the Walker Ground in Southgate, Middlesex openers Mike Gatting and Justin Langer made the most of the perfect batting conditions in a County Championship match against Essex, when they posted the highest first-class opening partnership in the club's history – a massive 372. The partnership was eventually broken when Langer fell for 166, caught by Rollins off the bowling of Ronnie Irani; Gatting went on to amass 241 runs before he too was eventually caught by Pritchard off the bowling of Danny Law.

SUNDAY 27th JUNE 2004

Middlesex's Simon Cook recorded his best ever List-A bowling figures for the club when he took six for 37 in a Totesport League match against Leicestershire at Grace Road, Leicester. Cook's return helped Middlesex dismiss Leicestershire for just 205 in their innings, with Middlesex reaching their required Duckworth Lewis adjusted target for the loss of four wickets, with Paul Weekes top-scoring for Middlesex with an innings of 90 in the six-wicket victory.

TUESDAY 27th JUNE 2006

Middlesex's record for the fifth wicket partnership in Twenty20 cricket was set when Scott Styris and Eoin Morgan put on 106 against Surrey at Lord's. Morgan scored 66 from 41 balls and hit six fours and three sixes, while Styris hit 56 from 34 balls and hit seven fours and one maximum. Despite the record, Middlesex could only post a total of 178 for 7 in reply to Surrey's 218 for 7, and lost the match by 40 runs.

SATURDAY 27th JUNE 2009

Playing a Twenty20 match against Surrey at the Brit Oval, Middlesex's number three, Owais Shah, and number four, Dawid Malan, put on a record third wicket partnership in Twenty20 cricket for Middlesex, with a stand of exactly 100. Shah finished on 61 not out from 41 balls, and Malan hit 38 from 35. Surrey had earlier scored a total of 160 in their 20 overs and, thanks to Shah and Malan, Middlesex cruised to their target for the loss of just three wickets to secure a valuable win over their London rivals.

MONDAY 28th JUNE 1926

Patsy Hendren became the first Middlesex player to take his place on the famous Lord's honours board for batting, when he converted an innings started on this day into a Test hundred for England against Australia in the second Ashes Test at Lord's. His innings of 127 not out in an England first-innings total of 475 for 3 declared helped England secure a draw in the match, in a series that England went on to win 1-0 and retain the Ashes.

SUNDAY 29th JUNE 2008

In a County Championship match against Northamptonshire, 20-year-old Roehampton-born Dawid Johannes Malan scored a first-class century on his debut for Middlesex at Park Road, Uxbridge. Malan's innings of 132 not out took Middlesex to a first-innings total of 340. As cricket invariably has a habit of doing, Malan was brought back down to earth with a bump, being dismissed for just 1 by Lance Klusener in the second innings.

THURSDAY 30th JUNE 1994

When a four-day County Championship match started at the County Ground in Derby, between Middlesex and Derbyshire, few there were to know that on the third day of the game, they would get to witness the finest bowling display by a Middlesex bowler in over 65 years. Richard Leonard Johnson became the only modern-day Middlesex bowler and only the fifth in the history of the club to take all ten opposition wickets in an innings, when he took 10 for 42 in just 18.5 overs, to secure a victory for Middlesex by an innings and 96 runs.

THURSDAY 30th JUNE 1977

One of the longest-standing records in List-A cricket is the record score by an opposition number seven batsman against Middlesex, which has been held for more than 30 years by Kent's John Shepherd, who smashed nine fours and two sixes on his way to 101 in a Kent total of 226. A tense run chase saw Mike Gatting pave the way for a Middlesex victory, with his 62 being the highest score in Middlesex's successful run chase, winning the game by eight wickets with just one ball to spare.

MIDDLESEX CCC
On This Day

JULY

SUNDAY 1st JULY 1990

A brilliant innings of 147 not out at Lord's against Worcestershire by Middlesex's Mark Ramprakash paved the way for a Middlesex total of 290 in their 40 overs and a victory over Hampshire by a margin of 99 runs. Ramprakash's innings was the fifth-highest ever List-A score by a Middlesex player.

FRIDAY 1st JULY 1994

In a match between Derbyshire and Middlesex at the County Ground in Derby, the extras column reached the heady heights of 81 runs when Derbyshire were bowling in the Middlesex first innings. This is the highest amount of extras that Middlesex have ever received in a first-class match, and included a staggering 54 no-balls. Derbyshire's bowling attack included England's Dominic Cork and Devon Malcolm – making the erratic display of bowling even more surprising.

TUESDAY 1st JULY 2003

Marley Richards, the son of legendary West Indian cricketer Viv Richards, joined up with the Middlesex squad to start a summer playing contract while studying at Oxford Brooks. The Middlesex squad of the day therefore contained younger relatives of three of the most celebrated cricketers the game has ever seen – Marley joined Denis Compton's grandson Nick, along with Sir Len Hutton's grandson Ben.

FRIDAY 1st JULY 2005

Owais Shah, with 79 runs, and Ed Smith, with 37, set a new record for the club's highest opening partnership in Twenty20 cricket, when they put on 100 for the first wicket against Essex at the Walker Ground in Southgate. Middlesex secured a victory in the match by posting a total of 185 for six in their 20 overs, before restricting Essex to 154 for seven to win by 31 runs.

SUNDAY 2nd JULY 1978

Norman Featherstone took his best ever List-A bowling figures of four for 10 against Worcestershire at New Road in a John Player League match. Featherstone's off spin helped to dismiss Worcestershire for just 134, but Middlesex collapsed and reached just 90 all out in their reply.

WEDNESDAY 2nd JULY 1980

South African Vintcent van der Bijl recorded his best ever List-A bowling figures for Middlesex when taking five for 12 off 10.4 overs against Ireland at Lord's. As a result, Ireland were dismissed for a total of just 102 in this Gillette Cup match, and Middlesex reached their target for the loss of five wickets with more than 21 overs to spare.

WEDNESDAY 2nd JULY 2008

Middlesex's wicketkeeping batsman, Ben James Matthew Scott, scored 164 not out in Middlesex's second innings of the County Championship match against Northamptonshire at Park Road, Uxbridge. Scott's innings set a new record for the highest individual score for a batsman at number eight in first-class cricket for Middlesex. His hundred wasn't enough to help Middlesex win the match though, as Northamptonshire hung on for a draw on the final day of the game.

FRIDAY 3rd JULY 1936

One of Middlesex's most elegant and classy batsmen, William (Eric) Russell, was born in Dumbarton, Scotland. Opening batsman Russell, whose Middlesex career spanned the years 1956 to 1972, was renowned for his fine late cuts and delicate leg glances. Russell is one of only a handful of Middlesex players to have surpassed 20,000 first-class runs for the club, scoring 23,103 runs at an average of 35.11, which included 37 hundreds in his 400 appearances for the county. For a decade and a half, Russell was widely regarded as one of the most stylish and accomplished opening batsmen in the country.

SATURDAY 3rd JULY 1982

Middlesex off-spinner Phil Edmonds bowled the club to a comfortable victory over Cheshire in the NatWest Bank Trophy first round, returning his best ever List-A bowling figures for Middlesex with five wickets for 12 runs from his 12 overs. Cheshire, having been torn apart by an Edmonds onslaught, recovered from 45 for seven before they were dismissed for a total of 104. Middlesex comfortably reached their target, losing only two wickets with more than eight overs to spare, with Wilf Slack top-scoring for Middlesex with a chanceless 54 not out.

SATURDAY 3rd JULY 1993

Phil Tufnell recorded career-best first-class bowling figures for Middlesex when taking eight for 29 against Glamorgan at Sophia Gardens, Cardiff in a County Championship match. Despite Glamorgan scoring a massive 562 in their first innings, with Vivian Richard hitting an unbeaten 224, Middlesex won the match convincingly by ten wickets, thanks to scoring 584 in their first innings with hundreds from Emburey (123) and Gatting (173). Tufnell knocked over Glamorgan for 109 in their second innings, leaving Middlesex a target of just 88 to win.

SUNDAY 4th JULY 2010

The margins of victory in Twenty20 cricket are often extremely slight, although this proved not to be the case at the County Ground in Taunton in this Friends Provident Twenty20 match. A rampant Somerset side destroyed Middlesex, dishing out their largest ever defeat in a Twenty20 match – by a huge 79 runs. Marcus Trescothick was the main antagonist, smashing 83 runs off just 38 balls, whilst James Hildreth (48 runs off 35 balls) and Arul Suppiah (26 off 16 balls) also added to the defeat. Somerset posted 204 in their 20 overs, before dismissing Middlesex for just 125.

MONDAY 5th JULY 1954

England's Test victory over Pakistan in the second Test match of the four-match series at Trent Bridge, Nottingham, will be remembered for one innings of brilliance by a Middlesex batsman. Denis Charles Scott Compton achieved the highest ever score by a Middlesex batsman when on Test duty with England, scoring a quite brilliant 278. His innings helped England to a first-innings total of 558 for 6 and set up an England victory. Compton's innings is still the eighth highest ever individual total scored by an English batsman, and remains the highest ever by a Middlesex player more than 60 years later.

WEDNESDAY 5th JULY 2000

Tim Bloomfield's best ever List-A bowling figures for Middlesex came in a comprehensive victory over Somerset at Southgate in the NatWest Trophy. His four for 17 off eight overs helped dismiss Somerset for just 58 in reply to Middlesex's total of 223.

FRIDAY 6th JULY 2007

Records galore were set in a Twenty20 Cup match at Lord's against Essex, as both Timothy James (Tim) Murtagh and Chad Blake Keegan entered the Middlesex record books, managing to score the highest ever individual scores for Middlesex batsmen batting at number nine and number ten respectively in Twenty20 cricket. Murtagh's innings of 40 not out came off just 24 balls, including six fours and one maximum, whilst Keegan's innings of 22 came off just 13 balls and saw him hit one four and one six. Also joining in the record-breaking antics was Middlesex's Indian overseas bowler, Murali Kartik, who became the first ever player to take a five-wicket haul in Twenty20 cricket for Middlesex with five for 13 off four overs. Middlesex's wicketkeeper, Ben James Matthew Scott, also joined in the fun, becoming the first Middlesex wicketkeeper to claim four victims in a Twenty20 innings. Despite so many club records being set in the game, Middlesex ended on the losing side, going down by three wickets as Essex chased down the Middlesex total of 126 with just one ball to spare.

MONDAY 7th JULY 1873

In a match between Middlesex and Marylebone Cricket Club at Lord's, Middlesex batsman ID Walker was batting in sublime form, and despatched a huge six into the recently-installed billiard room situated within the Lord's pavilion during his innings of 40 in Middlesex's first innings. Despite scoring 40 in both innings, Walker was unable to stop MCC winning the match by 84 runs.

WEDNESDAY 8th JULY 1998

At the Walker Ground in Southgate, Middlesex number ten Richard Leonard Johnson, a player far better known for his bowling performances, defied his batting average of just 11 and came to the fore with a record-breaking innings in a NatWest Bank Trophy match against Durham. His innings came when Middlesex were in dire trouble, at 178 for eight, chasing a Durham total of 240. In just 27 balls he smashed 45 not out, including six boundaries, to see Middlesex to 244 for eight, winning the match with eight balls to spare. Johnson's innings remains the highest ever List-A score by a Middlesex number ten batsman.

TUESDAY 8th JULY 2008

Dawid Johannes Malan shot to cricketing notoriety when playing for Middlesex in the quarter-final of the 2008 Twenty20 Cup against Lancashire. When Middlesex qualified for the quarter-finals and earned a home tie, the match had to be hastily moved to Surrey's Brit Oval, with Lord's being unavailable due to international match commitments. Batting first, Middlesex were in deep trouble at 21 for four when Malan came to the crease at number six. Of the 54 balls he faced, he despatched six of them into the stands and ten to the boundary, blitzing his way to a match-winning score of 103 and to a Middlesex total of 176 from their 20 overs. With Lancashire only reaching 164 in reply, Middlesex won the game by 12 runs and qualified for finals day at the Rose Bowl.

WEDNESDAY 9th JULY 1817

A first-class match involving Middlesex did take place nearly half a century before the official foundation of Middlesex County Cricket Club as we know it today, and it was a particularly strange match to say the very least. A Marylebone Cricket Club side, which included 22 players, took on a Middlesex side with the slightly more conventional 11 players in it. Despite the mismatch in numbers, Middlesex scored 165 in their first innings, and then took 21 wickets to dismiss MCC for 107. Middlesex followed this up with 168 in their second innings, before dismissing MCC again for just 161, to record a 55-run victory. No completed scorecard of the match exists, but Middlesex bowler John Bentley is credited with taking 15 of the 42 MCC wickets taken in the match.

WEDNESDAY 9th JULY 1997

No Middlesex batsman has ever scored a century and taken five wickets in a List-A match in the club's history, but South African Jacques Henry Kallis came close in a NatWest Bank Trophy match against Gloucestershire at Park Road, Uxbridge. Kallis took four of the Gloucestershire wickets for 47 runs, as the visitors reached 277 in their 60 overs, before he scored a fine century (100), paving the way for a four-wicket Middlesex victory which was reached with just three balls to spare.

SATURDAY 10th JULY 2010

In a Friends Provident Twenty20 match against Hampshire at Uxbridge, Middlesex batsman Owais Shah's innings of 80 set a new club record for the highest ever score by a Middlesex number three batsman in Twenty20 cricket. His innings included five fours, five sixes and came off just 52 balls. Despite Shah's efforts Hampshire secured a six-wicket victory, reaching their target of 165 with nine balls to spare.

TUESDAY 11th JULY 2006

Johann Louw returned the third-best ever bowling figures in Twenty20 cricket for Middlesex when he took 4 for 18 against Hampshire at the Walker Ground in Southgate. Louw's spell helped Middlesex dismiss Hampshire for just 111, which Middlesex reached in fourteen overs, one wicket down, with Nick Compton scoring 50.

TUESDAY 11th JULY 1893

The club's seventh-highest first-class wicket taker of all time, Frederick John (Jack) Durston was born in Clophill, Bedfordshire. Durston is one of only nine bowlers to have taken more than 1,000 first-class wickets for Middlesex, taking 1,178 wickets at an average of 21.96. Durston led Middlesex's pace attack in the Championship-winning sides of 1920 and 1921 which led to a Test call-up by England. Despite taking five for 136 on his Test debut, he was surprisingly dropped from the side, never to play for his country again.

MONDAY 12th JULY 1869

Surrey only had themselves to blame for losing a County match against Middlesex at Lord's – they played the entire game with only ten men. Batting first, Middlesex were dismissed for just 96, but managed to bowl out Surrey for a meagre 37 runs in their first innings. Middlesex struggled in their second innings, being bowled out for 89, leaving Surrey a target of just 149 to win. Under the circumstances, their total of 105 was creditable, and they lost by 43 runs. Had Surrey played 11 men in the match this may well have helped, as Frederick Buckle was simply listed as 'absent' on the scorecard of both Surrey innings. He arrived too late to bat in the first innings, and declared himself too ill to bat in the second.

WEDNESDAY 12th JULY 1876

In a County match between Middlesex and Nottinghamshire at the Princes Ground, Chelsea, Middlesex escaped with a draw in bizarre and tragic circumstances, as the death of veteran cricketer Thomas Box caused the match to be immediately halted. With Notts needing only 55 runs in their second innings to win the game, they had reached ten for one when, while attending the score board, Box collapsed and subsequently died at the ground, leaving Notts just 45 runs short of victory.

SATURDAY 12th JULY 1986

Middlesex once again reached the Benson and Hedges Cup final, their third in just over a decade. Kent were the opponents at Lord's as Mike Gatting looked to add to the two one-day trophies he had already successfully led the side to. Kent captain Chris Cowdrey put Middlesex in to bat and, despite losing the early wicket of Wilf Slack, Middlesex bounced back to post a reasonable, albeit under par total of 199 from their 55 overs. Once again Clive Radley shone in the final, top-scoring for Middlesex with a fine 54. In reply Kent got off to a disastrous start, losing their first three wickets to the pace of Daniel and Cowans with just 20 runs on the board. A recovery of sorts was mustered, but man of the match John Emburey and spin partner Phil Edmonds swung the game Middlesex's way as Kent were dismissed for 197, just three runs short of their 200 target.

TUESDAY 13th JULY 1976

Having only ever lost a first-class match by one run once in their entire history, Middlesex repeated the unfortunate feat against Yorkshire at Park Avenue Cricket Ground, Bradford. In a low scoring and evenly matched affair, parity reigned in the first innings, with Yorkshire posting 228 and Middlesex 206. Yorkshire's second innings continued in the same vein, with the home side being dismissed for 214, leaving Middlesex with a target of 237 for victory. When Mike Brearley hit 44, Norman Featherstone 78 and Mike Gatting 40, Middlesex looked to have got home, but a late collapse which saw them lose their last three wickets for just five runs saw Middlesex dismissed for 235 to lost the match by a run.

TUESDAY 14th JULY 1868

At Bramall Lane, Sheffield, in a county match against Middlesex, Yorkshire's captain on the day, Roger Iddison, instilled so much faith in his opening bowlers, George Freeman and Thomas Emmett, that they bowled unchanged for the entirety of both Middlesex innings. In the match, Freeman bowled 52 overs, taking 12 for 61, and from the other end Emmett bowled 51 overs, taking six for 58. While not necessarily in the best spirit of the game, Iddison's tactics were certainly effective, as Middlesex were dismissed for 79 in their first innings and just 59 in their second. Yorkshire ran out winners in the match by an innings and 24 runs, having posted 162 in their first and only innings.

FRIDAY 15th JULY 2005

After consistently impressing for his native Ireland, Middlesex batsman Edmund Christopher (Ed) Joyce switched allegiances and officially qualified to play for England on this day, after a meeting with the ICC clarified his qualification to play for the country. Despite a glittering first-class and List-A career with Middlesex, Joyce was never picked to play Test cricket for England, and had to satisfy himself instead with 17 One-Day International and two International Twenty20 appearances. Ironically, five years after qualifying for England, Joyce switched back to Ireland, looking to build on the 50-plus caps that he had received earlier in his career. Joyce's about turn and subsequent availability saw him selected for Ireland in the 2011 ICC World Cup, where he played in an historic victory over Andrew Strauss's England side.

FRIDAY 16th JULY 2010

With two matches remaining in their 2010 Friends Provident Twenty20 campaign, anything less than two wins would see Middlesex eliminated from the competition. With this in mind at the Rose Bowl, Middlesex set about destroying the Hampshire batting line-up, dismissing them for the lowest ever total scored against a Middlesex side in Twenty20 cricket – just 99, with only three Hampshire batsmen making double figures. Middlesex knocked off the runs with plenty of time to spare, reaching their target inside 15 overs to secure a vital win. Despite also beating Essex in their final group game, Middlesex suffered an agonising elimination by virtue of a lower net run rate to the side that they beat so comfortably at the Rose Bowl.

MONDAY 17th JULY 1911

Frank Tarrant was well known for his all-round talents in first-class cricket, and in a County Championship match starting on this day against Hampshire he scored a century for Middlesex with the bat and took five wickets with the ball. Amazingly, Tarrant achieved the 'all rounders' feat on nine separate occasions. Against Hampshire he scored 112 when opening in the Middlesex first innings, before then taking five for 42 in Hampshire's second innings as Middlesex secured a convincing 122-run victory.

THURSDAY 17th JULY 1919

Middlesex posted their highest ever first-class-innings total against near neighbours and London rivals, Surrey, at the Kennington Oval. The Middlesex total of 568 for nine declared in their first innings included centuries from opener Henry Lee (163), number three John Hearne (113) and number four Eric Kidd (100). Henry Lee followed this up with another hundred in Middlesex's second innings, in a total of 193 for five declared, before Surrey hung on for the draw in the fourth innings of the match, scoring 245 for one, with Donald Knight scoring a century for the home side.

SUNDAY 17th JULY 2005

There was little more that Paul Weekes could have done to try and win a Totesport League match for Middlesex against Gloucestershire at the Walker Ground in Southgate. In a brilliant all-round performance, he scored 81 with the bat and then took four for 58 with the ball. Despite his efforts though, Middlesex lost the game by 4 wickets.

MONDAY 18th JULY 1988

Middlesex's West Indian opening batsman, Wilf Norris Slack, became only the second person in the club's history to post an unbeaten century in both innings of a first-class match during a County Championship fixtures against Glamorgan at Lord's. He followed up his 163 not out in the Middlesex first-innings total of 420 for three declared with a fine 105 not out in the second-innings total of 195 for one declared. Despite this incredible effort from Slack, Glamorgan were able to secure a draw in the match.

SUNDAY 18th JULY 1993

Middlesex's opening batsman Desmond Haynes was at his absolute best against Warwickshire at Edgbaston in an AXA Equity and Law League match, when he single-handedly took apart the Warwickshire bowlers and scored 142 not out in a Middlesex total of 261 for two. Mike Roseberry stayed with Haynes initially and the pair of them put on 175 for the opening wicket, before Roseberry fell for 66. In a rain reduced match which saw Warwickshire only receiving 49 overs, they managed to reach 253 for eight – just eight runs short of Middlesex's total. They lost by the narrowest of margins by virtue of a slower run scoring rate, but Haynes's score is still the eighth-highest individual-innings total in List-A cricket by a Middlesex player.

SUNDAY 18th JULY 1999

At the Arundel Castle Cricket Ground in a CGU National League match, Sussex captain Chris Adams set a new record for the highest ever score for an opposition number three batsman in List-A cricket against Middlesex, scoring 163 runs in a Sussex total of 297. Middlesex's run chase came close to reaching their target, but fell just nine runs short on 288, with Owais Shah top-scoring for Middlesex with a brilliant innings of 134, the ninth-highest List-A score ever by a Middlesex player.

SATURDAY 19th JULY 1975

Middlesex's first one-day domestic final appearance came in the final of the Benson and Hedges Cup in 1975, where Leicestershire were the opponents at Lord's. Led by captain Mike Brearley, Middlesex won the toss and chose to bat, opening up with Mike Smith and Phil Edmonds. Edmonds smashed the second ball of the match for six, but fell shortly after for 11, as did the rest of the Middlesex batting line-up. Only Smith, who made 83, came out of the innings with any pride intact, with the extras column, making 13, being the second-highest scorer on the Middlesex batting card as they were dismissed for just 146. In reply only Fred Titmus made any real impact on the Leicestershire batsmen, taking two for 30, but they made easy work of the run chase, reaching 150 inside 52 overs to secure a five-wicket victory and pick up the first trophy of the season.

THURSDAY 20th JULY 1865

In a county match starting on this day between Middlesex and Lancashire at Old Trafford, Manchester, Vyell Edward Walker – the fifth of seven cricket-playing brothers within the famous Walker family who were instrumental in establishing Middlesex CCC – made his mark in history by becoming the first ever Middlesex bowler to take ten opposition wickets in an innings in the Lancashire second innings. His figures of 44.2 overs, five maidens, ten for 104 are even more remarkable when you consider that his bowling action is described in cricketing archives as 'slow right arm underarm'. Furthermore, as captain, he didn't even give himself a bowl in the Lancashire first innings.

MONDAY 20th JULY 1998

Only three players in history have taken a hat-trick against Middlesex in the club's List-A history, and the most unlikely of them all must surely be Sussex's Chris Adams – much better known for his prowess with the bat. In an AXA League match at the County Ground in Hove, Adams accounted for Richard Johnson, David Goodchild and Alistair Fraser on his way to taking five for 16 and recording his best ever List-A bowling figures. Middlesex lost the match by six wickets.

TUESDAY 21st JULY 1888

Twenty-three years on nearly to the day since the feat was last achieved, Middlesex's George Burton became only the second Middlesex bowler in the club's history to take all ten opposition wickets in a first-class innings. The unfortunate batsmen on this occasion were all from Surrey, in a County Championship match at the Kennington Oval, as Burton dismissed the entire team for a first-innings total of 163, to claim bowling figures of ten for 59 off 52.3 overs. Despite his best efforts, Surrey went on to claim a three-wicket victory in the match.

SUNDAY 21st JULY 1991

Middlesex lost a Refuge Assurance League match to Lancashire at Lord's, despite Norman Cowans delivering the fourth-best List-A bowling figures in the club's history. Cowans took six wickets for just nine runs in eight overs, but Lancashire still managed to pass the winning line, scoring 147 for eight in reply to Middlesex's earlier total of 143.

SUNDAY 22nd JULY 1973

Middlesex's Dennis Marriott can consider himself extremely unlucky to finish on the losing side in a John Player League match against Gloucestershire at the Recreational Trust Ground in Lydney. Marriott came on as the fifth bowler for Middlesex, and in 7.5 overs recorded his best ever List-A figures as he claimed the last five Gloucestershire wickets for just 13 runs. Middlesex dismissed Gloucestershire for just 113 runs – at less than three an over Middlesex should have cruised to victory, but they collapsed in fine style and were bowled out for a meagre 48 in 30.1 overs to lose the match by a staggering 65 runs.

TUESDAY 22nd JULY 1977

An exhausted Phil Edmonds completed his 77th over of bowling for Middlesex against Gloucestershire at Lord's on the third day of a County Championship match, handing him the record of delivering the highest amount of balls ever bowled in an innings by a Middlesex bowler, some 462 balls. This marathon effort saw Edmonds finish the innings with figures of eight for 132.

THURSDAY 22nd JULY 1993

John Emburey recorded his best ever first-class bowling figures for Middlesex in a County Championship match at Lord's, when he took eight for 40 in the Hampshire second innings, as the visitors were bowled out for just 88. Hampshire had earlier made 280 in their first innings, in which Emburey also took four for 75, and Middlesex made 310 in theirs, so just 59 runs were needed for victory. Middlesex won by nine wickets, and Emburey finished with figures of 12 for 115 in the match.

SATURDAY 23rd JULY 1949

Opening batsman John David Benbow (Jack) Robertson recorded the highest ever individual innings by a Middlesex batsman, with 331 not out, on the opening day of a County Championship match versus Worcestershire at New Road. His amazing individual score, which included 39 fours and two sixes, formed part of a Middlesex total of 623 for five declared, which was Middlesex's sixth-highest ever first-class innings total. They secured victory by the huge margin of an innings and 54 runs.

SATURDAY 23rd JULY 1983

Middlesex reached their second Benson and Hedges Cup final eight years after their first one, which had finished in a disappointing loss to Leicestershire. This time, however, Middlesex were on top of the County Championship under the leadership of Mike Gatting. Essex were also flying high, but Middlesex came into the game as slight favourites. A damp Lord's on the day of the final led to Essex captain Keith Fletcher putting Middlesex in to bat. They never really recovered from a slow start, and were in deep trouble at 74 for four at one point. Only Clive Radley really got on top of the Essex attack, scoring a magnificent 89 not out in extremely testing conditions. The Middlesex innings closed on just 196 from their 55 overs. Essex got off to an absolute flyer and looked to be cruising to victory at 71 without loss after ten overs. They looked to be home and dry as the innings progressed, but a four-wicket haul from Norman Cowans and some controlled bowling from Emburey and Edmonds turned the tide Middlesex's way. Needing just 12 runs to win with four overs and three wickets remaining, Essex were dismissed for 192, five runs short of their target, to give Middlesex their first ever Benson and Hedges Cup victory.

MONDAY 24th JULY 1933

Middlesex's Elias Henry (Patsy) Hendren's first-innings score of 301 not out set a new record for the highest individual first-class score for any batsman batting at number four for Middlesex. It came in a County Championship encounter with Worcestershire at Tipton Road, Dudley, in a Middlesex total of 591 for six declared. Despite Hendren's efforts the match ended in a draw as Worcestershire posted scores of 262 and 176 for five in reply.

FRIDAY 24th JULY 2009

Middlesex's Tim Murtagh recorded his career-best first-class bowling figures when playing for Middlesex in the County Championship against Derbyshire at the County Ground, Derby. Murtagh's wicket haul of seven for 82 from 22 overs surpassed the seven for 95 he had taken the previous year, but was not enough to secure a win for Middlesex, as the game finished in a draw on the final day of the match.

MONDAY 25th JULY 1864

Despite this being the first ever first-class fixture played by Middlesex at the current Lord's Cricket Ground, it was a far from auspicious start to life in the ground that was eventually to become Middlesex's permanent home. Taking on Marylebone Cricket Club, Middlesex were dismissed for their lowest team total ever of just 20 runs. Marylebone Cricket Club only used two bowlers, Grundy and Wootton, who took five wickets apiece, for ten and eight runs respectively, with the other two runs on the total being leg byes. Middlesex's number nine, Isaac D Walker, top-scored with just seven runs. With MCC scoring 113 in reply, and Middlesex 154 in their second attempt, MCC reached a winning score of 63 for the loss of five wickets.

THURSDAY 26th JULY 1866

Middlesex's George Howitt had an incredible match at the Cattle Market Ground, Islington, as he had a hand in taking all ten of Surrey's wickets in their first innings. Dismissed for just 108, Howitt claimed seven Surrey wickets with his bowling, taking seven for 38 off his 29 overs. Not wanting to give up his place in the spotlight, he then took the three catches that accounted for the other remaining Surrey wickets. Howitt's efforts ensured that Middlesex went on to secure a comfortable win, by an innings and 172 runs.

SATURDAY 26th JULY 2008

Middlesex were crowned Twenty20 champions following a thrilling last-ball victory over Kent on finals day at the Rose Bowl in Hampshire. In the semi-final, underdogs Middlesex qualified for the final by chasing down the target of 139, set by favourites Durham, for the loss of just two wickets, thanks largely to an amazing innings of 59 from just 21 balls from big-hitting South African Tyron Henderson, including seven huge sixes. In the final, Middlesex posted a huge total of 187 batting first, with Owais Shah smashing 75 from just 35 deliveries. In reply, it came down to Kent needing just three runs from the final two deliveries of the match. Tyron Henderson delivered a deadly accurate yorker for the penultimate ball, then ran out Kent's Justin Kemp on the final ball of the match to secure Middlesex their first silverware in 15 years.

WEDNESDAY 27th JULY 1960

Playing for Middlesex in a County Championship fixture at the Town Ground, Northampton, Alan Moss recorded his best ever first-class bowling figures for Middlesex. Northants made 225 in their first innings, with Moss taking three for 60, and in reply Middlesex managed 297 in theirs. In Northamptonshire's second innings, however, Moss destroyed the visitors' batting line-up and took eight for 31 from 21 overs to record his career-best figures. Northants made just 58 runs, and Middlesex secured a win without having to bat again, by an innings and 14 runs.

MONDAY 27th JULY 1868

History was made for Middlesex in a County Championship match against Kent at the Cattle Market Ground, Islington, when Thomas Hearne became the first bowler to claim a hat-trick for the club. It came in the Kent second innings and the fourth innings of the game, with Kent needing 276 to win. First to fall was George Remnant, who was clean bowled by Hearne for 13. He followed this by clean bowling Kent's number seven batsman, Charles Payne, first ball for 0, before completing the feat when George 'Farmer' Bennett came to the crease and promptly lobbed a catch up to Russell Walker to follow Payne back to the pavilion for a first-ball duck. Kent were dismissed for just 103, with Hearne taking three wickets for just six runs off 11 overs to see Middlesex to a 172-run victory.

WEDNESDAY 28th JULY 1976

Middlesex have only lost once in their history when forcing an opponent to follow on in a match, and Kent were the beneficiaries on that occasion at Hesketh Park, Dartford. Batting first, Middlesex posted a total of 305 before dismissing Kent for just 151, so Middlesex captain Mike Brearley quite rightly took the initiative and put Kent in again. At this point the fortunes of both sides turned, as Kent proceeded to knock up 348 in their second innings. Even then, this only left Middlesex needing 195 to win. Graham Johnson (5-40) and Derek Underwood (4-39) had other ideas, as they ripped through the Middlesex batting with a brilliant display of spin bowling. Middlesex were bowled out for just 137, with Kent winning the match by a staggering 57 runs.

SATURDAY 29th JULY 1905

In a County Championship match against Essex at Lord's, Middlesex captain Pelham 'Plum' Warner made a decision that he came to regret, declaring Middlesex's second innings early in an attempt to force a result in Middlesex's favour. With a first-innings lead of 101 already in the bag, Middlesex had reached 152 for three when Warner pulled the team in and declared the Middlesex second innings closed. Essex then proceeded to score the required 254 runs with some ease for the loss of only three wickets, leading to some harsh criticism of Warner's declaration decision. In response to his critics, Warner simply quoted: "Tis better to have declared and lost, than never to have played at all."

TUESDAY 29th JULY 1997

In a NatWest Trophy quarter-final match against Warwickshire, Middlesex's bowlers set a new club record for the highest amount of extras that Middlesex have ever conceded in a List-A match. They very generously gave away a huge 47 extras in the match, which proved vital to the result as Warwickshire won the match by 28 runs and qualified for the semi-finals. Of the 47 extras that Middlesex delivered, 16 were leg byes, 11 were no-balls and 20 were wides.

MONDAY 30th JULY 1906

Only twice in Middlesex's history has a fielder achieved the feat of taking six catches in an opponents' innings. Frank Tarrant became the first Middlesex player to do so in a County Championship fixture against Essex at the County Ground, Leyton. Middlesex bowler Guy Napier had a lot to thank Tarrant for, as Tarrant took four of his six catches off Napier's bowling, with the other two coming off Edward Mignon.

THURSDAY 30th JULY 1908

Frank Tarrant delivered one of the finest first-class all-round performances ever for Middlesex in a County Championship match against Gloucestershire at Bristol. Tarrant scored 152 in Middlesex's first innings before taking seven for 93 in Gloucestershire's first innings, then took five for 56 in their second. He finished with match figures of 12 for 149, but Middlesex still only just won the match by two runs.

MONDAY 31st JULY 1899

One of the longest standing and most widely discussed records in the cricket history books was set at Lord's by an Australian, Albert Edwin Trott. Middlesex's Trott entered the record books when he smashed a delivery from Australian Monty Noble clean over the Lord's pavilion for six to achieve a feat managed by no other batsman in history. The huge blow from Trott was confirmed as clearly having gone over the pavilion roof, as the ball was recovered from the garden of Philip Need, the Lord's dressing room attendant, who resided behind the pavilion. Trott's clean hitting was the stuff of legends – remarkably, he would have set the record two months earlier had the ball he hit not struck the cornicing of the South Turret of the Lord's pavilion, which is approximately 15 feet higher than the roof he actually cleared. In 2011, in a sponsorship stunt, bat maker Mongoose offered Somerset's Marcus Trescothick £1million if he can repeat Trott's feat, in any one-day game.

THURSDAY 31st JULY 1930

Middlesex leg spin and googly bowler Ian Peebles took his best ever first-class bowling figures for Middlesex in a County Championship match against Worcestershire at New Road, recording eight for 24 in the Worcestershire second innings. This marked the end of a great week for Peebles, as he had caused the great Don Bradman so many difficulties in the fourth Test match at Old Trafford the previous week that Bradman had declared publicly that he had found Peebles' bowling to be close to unplayable. Peebles also took five for 48 in the Worcestershire first innings to finish the match with brilliant figures of 13 for 72.

MONDAY 31st JULY 1933

In a County Championship match at Queens Park, Chesterfield against Derbyshire, two Middlesex bowlers took apart the home side's batting line-up in both innings to secure a convincing victory for Middlesex. In the Derbyshire first innings Jim Sims achieved the second-best first-class bowling figures of his career when taking eight for 47 to dismiss them for just 167, before 'Young Jack' Hearne achieved the best bowling figures of his own career, taking nine for 61 as Derbyshire were knocked over for just 175. Middlesex won the game by eight wickets.

MIDDLESEX CCC
On This Day

AUGUST

MONDAY 1st AUGUST 1864

Middlesex's opener, Thomas Hearne, took his place in the club's history books by becoming the first Middlesex player to score a century for the county. His innings of 125 came at the Cattle Market Ground, Islington, against Marylebone Cricket Club, in a Middlesex total of 411. He followed his fine innings up with four for 49 to dismiss MCC for just 93 in their first innings, and then three for 42 in their second innings of just 86, as Middlesex won by an innings and 232 runs. Hearne just beat Middlesex's number five to the honour, as Thomas Case also reached three figures in the Middlesex first innings, scoring 116.

THURSDAY 1st AUGUST 1907

Frank Tarrant, one of only nine bowlers to ever take more than 1,000 first-class wickets for Middlesex, took his best ever career bowling figures for the club during a County Championship match against Gloucestershire at the Ashley Down Ground in Bristol. Tarrant took nine for 41 from 15 overs to dismiss Gloucestershire for just 69 to secure a Middlesex win by an innings and 140 runs. Tarrant took nine opposition wickets on five separate occasions for Middlesex in first-class matches.

SUNDAY 1st AUGUST 1937

Middlesex beat Sussex at the County Ground in Hove in their largest ever innings margin victory in a first-class match. Batting first, Sussex were dismissed for just 101 before Middlesex batted and scored a huge 632 for eight in their first innings, with hundreds from Patsy Hendren (187) and John Human (125) to lead by 531 runs. The Somerset second innings showed signs of improvement, but they were dismissed for just 180 to lose by a margin of an innings and 351 runs.

WEDNESDAY 1st AUGUST 1984

Middlesex batsman Graham Derek Barlow recorded the highest ever List-A score for a Middlesex player batting at number one when he was run out for 158 against Lancashire at Lord's in a NatWest Bank Trophy match. Barlow helped Middlesex post a total of 276 for eight in their 60 overs, which Lancashire never got close to, being dismissed for just 105 inside 30 overs.

SATURDAY 2nd AUGUST 1975

Well over 20 Middlesex batsmen have achieved the feat of scoring a century in both innings of a first-class match for the club, but only two players in history have done it with unbeaten centuries. Norman Featherstone became the first to do so, when he played against Kent in a County Championship fixture at the St Lawrence Ground, Canterbury. He scored an unbeaten 127 in a first-innings total of 430, which he followed up with an unbeaten 100 in a Middlesex second-innings total of 180. His endeavours were to good effect, as Middlesex won the game by 156 runs.

WEDNESDAY 3rd AUGUST 1977

In a Gillette Cup quarter-final match at Lord's, Middlesex batsmen Michael John Smith and Clive Thornton Radley compiled the highest ever second wicket partnership for the club in List-A cricket, collectively putting on 223 against Hampshire. Smith led the way with 123 runs, and Radley scored a fine 94. Their partnership set Middlesex on their way to a total of 248 for three, chasing down the Hampshire total of 247 to secure a convincing seven-wicket victory.

WEDNESDAY 4th AUGUST 1886

At the age of 23, Middlesex player Andrew Ernest Stoddart scored a then-record individual-innings total of 485 during Hampstead's match against the Stoics. According to records, Stoddart's preparation the night before the game involved him taking in an evening of dancing, then embarking upon a card session which took him through to dawn, before setting off for the game at Hampstead Cricket Club. His unconventional pre-match build-up clearly worked, as he helped take the home side's score to a phenomenal 370 for three at lunch in just 150 minutes. He then continued batting throughout the day, for a total of six hours and ten minutes, hitting one eight, three fives and 64 fours in his massive score. The Hampstead innings closed with their total on a colossal 813. By all accounts, after the match, he went straight to play a tennis match, then went to the theatre, and eventually retired to bed at 3am the next morning for a well-earned rest.

MONDAY 5th AUGUST 1728

The earliest known reference to a team called 'Middlesex' played their first cricket fixture at a venue which is described as "in the fields behind the Woolpack, in Islington, near Sadler's Wells". They played against a team called the London Cricket Club, reportedly for a wager of £50 a side to the winners – the result is unknown.

THURSDAY 5th AUGUST 1993

Angus Fraser recorded his career best first-class bowling figures for Middlesex when he took seven for 40 in the Leicestershire first innings, as the visitors were dismissed for just 114 at Lord's in the County Championship. Batting first, Middlesex made a huge 551, with 185 from Mike Roseberry and 121 from Mike Gatting. Forced to follow on, Gloucestershire were dismissed for just 253 to lose by an innings and 184 runs. Fraser took one for 56 in the Leicestershire second innings to finish with match figures of eight for 96.

MONDAY 6th AUGUST 1900

In a County Championship match against Somerset at the County Ground in Taunton, Middlesex bowler Albert Edwin Trott became only the third player in the club's history to take all ten opposition wickets in an innings. His figures of ten for 42 in 14.2 overs with five maidens remain the second-best bowling figures in the history of the club, even to this day. He bowled unchanged from one end, with JT Hearne doing the same from the other end, without success. Trott's ten-wicket haul saw Somerset dismissed for 89 and set up a one-wicket victory for Middlesex.

TUESDAY 7th AUGUST 1956

In a County Championship match against Sussex at the County Ground in Hove, Don Bennett recorded his best ever bowling figures for Middlesex when he took seven for 47 from 17.4 overs. Sussex were bowled out for just 120 in their first innings, to which Middlesex made 271 in reply. Bennett also took two for 37 in the Sussex second innings of 197 to collect match bowling figures of nine for 84. Needing just 47 to win, Middlesex knocked off the runs for the loss of only one wicket.

FRIDAY 7th AUGUST 1992

Neil Williams recorded his career best first-class bowling figures for Middlesex when taking eight for 75 from 22.5 overs, as Gloucestershire were bowled out for 141 in their second innings in a County Championship fixture at Lord's. He also took four for 64 from 26 overs in the Gloucestershire first innings of 322, to finish with match figures of 12 for 139. Having scored 251 in their first innings, Middlesex were set a target of 213 runs to win in the fourth innings, which they reached for the loss of five wickets, with John Carr top-scoring with 66 for Middlesex.

FRIDAY 7th AUGUST 2009

A poor season for Middlesex which promised much but failed to deliver saw the club sat rock bottom of the division two table, having gone nine County Championship matches without a single win. They had to wait until this day before achieving their opening first-class win of the season, which they ironically achieved inside three days against a table-topping Kent side. Aside from poor form in the County Championship this year, Middlesex also lost their first seven Twenty20 Cup fixtures in defence of the crown they won in 2008. Middlesex's match against Kent was won in convincing fashion as, with Kent set an improbable 335 to win in the fourth innings, they were dismissed for 287. Murali Kartik's match figures of seven for 85 were a key factor in Middlesex's securing their first win of the season.

SUNDAY 8th AUGUST 1965

Middlesex's current managing director of cricket, Angus Robert Charles (Gus) Fraser, was born in Billinge, Wigan, Lancashire. Fraser was the stalwart of the Middlesex pace attack throughout a career which ran from 1984 until 2002, and he took 679 wickets at an average of 26.41, with best bowling figures of 7-40. Fraser captained the Middlesex side in 2001 and in his retirement year of 2002. He was voted Wisden's Cricketer of the Year in 1996 and represented England at Test level on 46 separate occasions, taking 177 wickets at 27.32, including taking eight wickets on two occasions, both against the West Indies – eight for 75 in Barbados in 1993/94 and eight for 53 in Port-of-Spain, Trinidad in 1997/98.

THURSDAY 9th AUGUST 1900

Just three days after taking all ten Somerset wickets in their first innings at Taunton, Albert Trott followed this up with another brilliant performance of accurate pace bowling, when he was instrumental in another victory for Middlesex in the County Championship. This time, against Gloucestershire at Clifton, he took five for 41 in the first innings and eight for 47 in the second, giving him match figures of 13 for 88 to confirm his position as one of the most feared and penetrative pace bowlers of his time.

TUESDAY 9th AUGUST 1904

When Middlesex's number ten batsman, Richard Edwardes More, started batting on the second day of this County Championship match against Yorkshire at Bramall Lane, Sheffield, little did everyone know what was to come. With Yorkshire looking to wrap up the Middlesex tail More dug in and batted his way to an unbeaten 120 to record the highest ever individual first-class total for a batsman batting in the number ten spot for Middlesex. His endeavours saved the game for the visitors.

TUESDAY 9th AUGUST 1993

Middlesex scored their highest ever first-class total against Essex when they scored 634 for seven declared at Chelmsford in the County Championship. Bowled out for just 83 in their first innings, Middlesex had Graham Barlow (132), Mike Gatting (160) and John Emburey (133) to thank for the huge second-innings total which saved the game for Middlesex and earned them a draw. Emburey's 133 was the highest first-class score of his career for Middlesex.

FRIDAY 10th AUGUST 1866

When playing against Nottinghamshire in a county match at Islington's Cattle Market Ground, Middlesex bowler Thomas Hearne had a strange encounter with a pigeon, which dive bombed him as he was running in to deliver the ball. Instead of bowling the ball towards the batsman, Hearne swung round and threw directly at the pigeon, hitting it full on and knocking it clean from the sky. He took the pigeon away with him after the game and had the bird stuffed and mounted. It sat as a trophy within his Ealing home thereafter.

SUNDAY 10th AUGUST 2003

Middlesex had number eight Simon James Cooke's record-breaking innings to thank for securing victory against Durham in a National League encounter at Lord's. In deep trouble at 66 for 6, Cooke strode to the crease on a mission! His innings of 67 not out from 66 balls set a new List-A record as the highest ever innings by a Middlesex number eight batsman and took Middlesex to a narrow 7-run victory. Cooke's match-winning innings was even more remarkable, given that his List-A batting average for Middlesex was just 16, and that he only scored fifty on one other occasion for Middlesex in a career which lasted seven years.

SUNDAY 11th AUGUST 2002

Playing against Northamptonshire in a Norwich Union League match, Middlesex were dismissed for their lowest ever List-A total at Lord's Cricket Ground. Having batted first, Northamptonshire posted a total of 286 for 7 in their 45 overs, with Australian Michael Hussey making a quite brilliant hundred. In reply, Middlesex lost both opening batsmen, Andrew Strauss and Ben Hutton (grandson of the late great Len Hutton) without a single run being added to the scoreboard. Things rarely improved at any point in the innings from thereafter, as Middlesex were skittled out for a mere 72 runs, to give Northants a massive 214-run victory, which also broke another club record, as the largest margin that Middlesex have ever lost a List-A match by.

FRIDAY 12th AUGUST 1867

Middlesex's worst season since the club was formed, and arguably their worst in history to this day, saw them go without a victory in any of the matches they played in, losing every single game bar one, when they managed a draw with neighbours Surrey at the Kennington Oval. They had club captain Vyell (VE) Walker to thank for their only draw of the season, as his 87 not out took Middlesex to a first-innings total of 249, in reply to Surrey's 243. Middlesex's season spoke for itself when the end-of-season club averages showed that only two batsmen had averaged more than 30 for the season – Bransby Cooper and Edward Tritton – and the leading wicket taker, Thomas Mantle, had taken just 16 first-class wickets all season.

SATURDAY 13th AUGUST 1887

Playing a county match at Fartown, Huddersfield against Yorkshire, Middlesex batsman Alexander Josiah Webbe carried his bat throughout the Middlesex second innings of 527 to score a magnificent 243 not out – the second-highest score in the club's history at the time – to set up the prospect of a brilliant third day's play. Sadly rain intervened, and no play was possible on the final day, so the players chose to play a football match out in the middle, to the immense entertainment of the crowd who had crammed into the ground to see the final day of the match. Sadly no record exists of the football match score, but the cricket match ended in a draw.

THURSDAY 14th AUGUST 1980

Middlesex paceman Wayne Daniel recorded the fifth-best List-A bowling figures in the history of the club when he took six for 15 against Sussex at the County Ground in Hove during a Gillette Cup match. His devastating spell of bowling helped dismiss Sussex for just 115, to see Middlesex win by 64 runs, having scored 179 runs in their innings. Daniel clearly enjoyed playing at Hove, having taken 6-17 there two years earlier.

MONDAY 14th AUGUST 1911

Middlesex opening batsman Francis Alfred Tarrant claimed the club record for the highest ever individual innings when carrying his bat through an all-out innings. His 207 not out, scored against Yorkshire at the Park Avenue Cricket Ground in Bradford, is still to this day the only double century ever achieved by a Middlesex batsman carrying his bat through an all-out innings. His innings came in a Middlesex first-innings total of 378, and Middlesex went on to draw the match.

MONDAY 15th AUGUST 2005

In a Totesport League match at Lord's, Paul Nicholas Weekes became the first and only Middlesex batsman to score four List-A centuries in a single season, when he scored 111 for the club against Northamptonshire. His innings of 111 runs came off 136 balls in a Middlesex total of 247, which fell just short of Northamptonshire's total of 261, leading to a win for the visitors by a 14-run margin.

TUESDAY 16th AUGUST 1977

John Emburey's off-spin accounted for eleven Northamptonshire wickets in a first-class County Championship encounter at the Wellingborough School Ground, yet despite this Middlesex suffered a heavy defeat in the match. Emburey took 5 for 27 from his 23.1 overs as Northants were bowled out for just 179 in their first innings. Middlesex however were then dismissed for their lowest ever-innings total against Northants, making just 62, as all but two batsmen made single figure scores. Emburey then took 6 for 84 as Northants pressed home their advantage and made 217 in their second innings, with Emburey's efforts to no avail, as Middlesex were then dismissed for 206 to lose the match by 128 runs.

THURSDAY 16th AUGUST 1990

When scoring 149 not out in the NatWest Trophy semi-final match against Lancashire at Old Trafford, West Indies and Middlesex opener, Desmond Leo Haynes, became the first ever and still the only Middlesex player to pass 1,000 List-A runs in a single season – a feat that no other batsman has ever achieved, yet Haynes also managed it in 1992. Despite scoring 296 in their innings, Middlesex lost the match by five wickets; however Haynes finished the season with a club record of 1,353 List-A runs to his name.

FRIDAY 17th AUGUST 1866

Playing against Cambridgeshire in a county match, a controversial incident involving Cambridgeshire's George Frederick Tarrant erupted. Tarrant refused to take his place at the batting crease in protest at the inclusion of Charles Newman, who had come into the side to replace the injured Robert Carpenter. Against Tarrant's name on the score sheet, it simply read 'Refused to go in'. Thomas Case, playing for Middlesex, is recorded as saying: "I very well remember seeing that spoilt child of fortune, who had been gifted with a miraculously fast delivery, but also with an entire absence of manners, lying down superciliously watching the match which he had deliberately done his best to ruin. Of such conduct it would be difficult to find a parallel in the annals of cricket." As a result of this incident, the Middlesex versus Cambridgeshire fixture was dropped for the following season, and despite a full apology from Tarrant and the club, Middlesex were not to play Cambridgeshire again for more than a hundred years.

SUNDAY 17th AUGUST 1969

A brilliant bowling performance by Middlesex's Ron Hooker in a Players County League match saw Middlesex cruise to victory over Surrey at Lord's by 129 runs. Hooker took an incredible six wickets for just six runs from eight overs as Surrey were dismissed for just 83 in 35.3 overs. Hooker's figures were at the time the best ever List-A figures for a Middlesex bowler, and even today they remain the third best bowling figures in the club's one-day history.

WEDNESDAY 17th AUGUST 1983

The great Ian Botham holds the record for the highest ever List-A score by an opposition number six batsman against Middlesex with 96 not out, which he scored in the NatWest Bank Trophy semi-final at Lord's. In a nail-biting match, Somerset drew level with the Middlesex score of 222 from the final ball of their innings, and progressed to the final having lost fewer wickets – eight compared to Middlesex's nine.

FRIDAY 18th AUGUST 1865

No official record stands for the longest six ever hit, largely as a result of many of them going unmeasured, but Surrey batsman George Griffith, playing at the Cattle Market Ground, Islington, against Middlesex, took a liking to Middlesex bowler Vyell Walker and smashed one of his 'underarm lobs' over the boundary, measured at a distance of 119 yards. Considering that any six above 100 yards is considered big in the modern game of today, where advances in cricket equipment have presumably made the feat that much easier, this was an incredible blow by Griffith.

WEDNESDAY 19th AUGUST 1925

Three times Middlesex captain (1935–38, 1946–47 and 1950) Walter Robins made his debut for Middlesex at the age of 19. Robins most famously captained the side through the hugely successful Compton and Edrich pre and post war eras of the 1930s and 1940s, in which he represented the county in 258 first-class matches. In his Middlesex career, Robins scored 9,337 first-class runs for the club at 26.37 and took 669 wickets at 22.28. As captain of Middlesex, Robins led the club to the Championship title in the infamous 1947 record-breaking season.

WEDNESDAY 20th AUGUST 1952

John Ernest Emburey, arguably the finest off-break bowler of his generation, was born in Peckham, South London. Emburey represented Middlesex between 1973 and 1995 and took an impressive 1,250 first-class wickets for Middlesex at an average of 24.09, the fifth-highest wicket haul in the club's history. Emburey formed a formidable bowling partnership with his fellow Middlesex spinner, Phil Edmonds, with the 'spin twins' often working in tandem for both club and country. Emburey was voted Wisden's Cricketer of the Year 1984 and played a total of 64 Test matches for England. Emburey's career best bowling figures were eight for 40 and he looks to have a place sat permanently in the Middlesex record books as the last bowler to take 100 wickets in a season, when he took 103 in 1983. It is highly unlikely that the feat will be repeated on the wickets prepared for the modern-day game.

FRIDAY 21st AUGUST 1868

A day of celebration for Middlesex fans and a proud day for the club as, in the final match of the season, they skittled out London rivals Surrey for just 35 runs in their second innings of this county match at the Cattle Market Ground, Islington. This constituted Surrey's lowest ever first-class total against Middlesex, which is a record they'll be thankful hasn't been beaten since, in nearly 150 years. In a match totally dominated by Middlesex, Surrey's batsmen had only managed to post a total of 89 in their first innings. Compared to their second attempt it was an outstanding effort, but it couldn't stop them losing heavily, by 171 runs, to Middlesex. The victors had scored 139 in their first innings and 156 in their second.

SUNDAY 22nd AUGUST 1999

In a CGU National League encounter with Northamptonshire at Lord's, David Charles Nash and Angus Fraser set a new record for the highest ever ninth wicket partnership for Middlesex in List-A matches. Nash finished with 40 not out and Fraser reached 31, before their partnership was broken on 73 runs. Their late-order heroics were not enough to save Middlesex, as Northamptonshire went on to win the game by five wickets.

SATURDAY 23rd AUGUST 1924

When Middlesex dismissed Gloucestershire for just 31 runs in their first innings at Greenbank in Bristol, it set a record as the lowest total ever scored against Middlesex in a first-class fixture. A highest score of seven for opener Fred Seabrook was the 'highlight' of their innings, with Nigel Haig taking six for 11 and Fred Durston four for 18 for Middlesex. Unbelievably, despite this, Gloucestershire won the match, scoring 294 in their second innings and bowling out Middlesex for 74 and 190, to win by 61 runs.

THURSDAY 23rd AUGUST 1984

Playing at Dean Park, Bournemouth, Phil Edmonds recorded the best ever first-class figures of his career with eight for 53 against Hampshire in the County Championship. Hampshire had earlier made only 188 in their first innings, with Edmonds taking four for 67, and Middlesex made 240 in reply. His eight wickets helped dismiss Hampshire for just 139 in their second innings, and Middlesex needed just 88 to win the match. They reached 91 for the loss of three wickets to win the game.

SUNDAY 24th AUGUST 1969

In a Players County League match at Lord's, Clive Thornton Radley posted the highest ever List-A score by a batsman batting at number two for Middlesex. Radley's innings of 133 not out came in a Middlesex total of 223 for six, which was enough to see them secure a 72-run victory over Glamorgan, who were dismissed for 151.

WEDNESDAY 24th AUGUST 1949

Middlesex started their final County Championship match of the season against Derbyshire, needing both a victory for them and a defeat for Yorkshire in their final match to stand any chance of winning the County Championship title – their second in three years. They duly obliged, although they trailed Derbyshire by 89 runs after both sides' first innings had been completed. Derbyshire then made just 103 in their second innings, leaving Middlesex a target of 193. While others around him struggled, Denis Compton's fine 97* took Middlesex to victory. With Yorkshire also winning however, both sides finished on equal points and had to settle for sharing the County Championship title.

SUNDAY 24th AUGUST 2003

In a high-scoring County Championship match at Old Trafford, Manchester, Middlesex scored their highest ever first-class-innings total against Lancashire with 544 runs in their first innings. Despite this, Middlesex were forced to follow on in the game, as Lancashire had posted a huge 734 for five in their first innings. In the Middlesex innings Andrew Strauss (155), Owais Shah (147) and Ben Hutton (107) each reached three figures. Trailing Lancashire by 180 runs, Middlesex had to follow on and reached 237 for seven to cling on for a draw.

MONDAY 25th AUGUST 1924

Having been dismissed for an all time low total of 31 in their first innings at Greenbank in Bristol, Gloucestershire pulled off an amazing recovery in the match to win by 61 runs. This was remarkable in itself, but another record was also broken on the match's final day. Gloucestershire's slow left-arm bowler, Charles Warrington Leonard (Charlie) Parker, entered the record books by becoming the only bowler in history to take a hat-trick in both innings against Middlesex in a first-class match. His hat-trick in the first innings came when he dismissed Richard Haynes Twining for just one, and then got the wickets of Gubby Allen and Frank Mann for first ball ducks, seeing Middlesex dismissed for just 74. He followed this up with a second-innings hat-trick by dismissing Mann again, John Guise and Nigel Haig, as Middlesex were dismissed for 190, to lose an incredible match.

WEDNESDAY 25th AUGUST 1982

Only one player in Middlesex's history has played in five separate decades. That honour, although achieved purely by chance, goes to Fred Titmus. Titmus was merely a spectator at Lord's in 1982, intending to sit and watch Middlesex's match against Surrey from the stands, when Middlesex's captain, Mike Brearley, called upon his talents one more time to play in the County Championship match on a slow turning wicket. Titmus duly obliged at the ripe old age of 49, some 33 years after making his debut on 25th June 1949, making history and securing Middlesex a vital victory in the process, taking three for 43 in the Surrey second innings, as they were dismissed for just 102 when needing only 161 for victory.

SATURDAY 25th AUGUST 2001

There have only been three first-class matches in history where four Middlesex batsmen have scored a hundred in the same innings, the most recent of which was against Warwickshire at Lord's. Winning the toss and electing to bat, Middlesex's innings of 502 for seven declared included centuries from Stephen Fleming (102), Ed Joyce (104), Paul Weekes (107) and David Nash (103). Despite this, Middlesex surprisingly didn't win the match. Mark Wagh scored an unbelievable 315 runs as Warwickshire hit 631 for nine declared in reply.

SATURDAY 26th AUGUST 1882

A day to forget as Middlesex suffered their largest ever first-class innings defeat at the hands of Lancashire in a match played at Old Trafford. Having posted a first-innings score of 439 all out, Lancashire then set about destroying the Middlesex batting line-up not once but twice, as Middlesex failed to reach three figures in either of their innings. They were bowled out for just 70 in the first innings and 98 in their second innings to suffer defeat by the massive margin of an innings and 271 runs.

MONDAY 27th AUGUST 1951

Middlesex's all time fourth-highest run scorer, John David Benbow (Jack) Robertson, became the first and only Middlesex player to score 25 half centuries in one season for the club, when scoring 70 not out against the touring South Africans at Lord's. Robertson had a season to remember, scoring a phenomenal 2,917 runs at 56.09.

FRIDAY 28th AUGUST 1903

Middlesex's first season as winners of the County Championship concluded with an innings victory over rivals Surrey at the Kennington Oval. Middlesex's inaugural season as County Championship winners saw them win eight of their 16 matches, drawing seven and losing just one, to Yorkshire, who were the dominant county side of the day having won the title in five of the previous seven seasons. Middlesex lifted the crown with an annihilation of Surrey by an innings and 94 runs. Having won the toss and batted first, Middlesex posted a total of 281 in their first innings before dismissing Surrey for 57 and 130, securing victory and the title inside two days.

SUNDAY 28th AUGUST 1994

In an AXA Equity and Law match against Surrey at the Kennington Oval, Middlesex were hopeful of victory having posted a total of 261 in their 40 overs, with Mike Roseberry top scoring with 119 not out. In reply, however, Alistair Brown made light work of the run chase, setting a new record for the highest ever individual score by a number two batsman against Middlesex in List-A cricket. He bludgeoned his way to 142 not out to see Surrey over the winning line with a couple of overs to spare.

TUESDAY 29th AUGUST 1882

Middlesex's Charles Thomas Studd and Alfred Lyttelton both played in the famous Test match at the Kennington Oval in the game that saw the birth of the Ashes. Australia, including the legend Fred 'the Demon' Spofforth, were seemingly down and out in the match, with England needing just 85 runs to win in their second innings. At 66 for four England appeared to have had the match won, but Spofforth and Boyle then bowled 16 consecutive maiden overs to apply huge pressure to England. Wicket after wicket then fell, including Lyttelton, who had made 12, but when Studd took his place at the crease England needed only ten runs to win the Test. Studd remained the not out batsman as the wickets of Barnes and Peate fell to give Australia an historic Test win over England. Australia's hero was Spofforth, who took 14 England wickets in the match. Reginald Brooks, a journalist with *The Sporting Times*, famously wrote the mock obituary: "In affectionate remembrance of ENGLISH CRICKET, which died at the Oval on 29th August 1882. Deeply lamented by a large circle of sorrowing friends and acquaintances – R.I.P. The body will be cremated and the ashes taken to Australia". Studd is named on an inscription on the original Ashes urn.

SATURDAY 29th AUGUST 1891

One of only two bowlers to have taken more than 2,000 first-class wickets for Middlesex, JT (Jack) Hearne recorded his best ever first-class career bowling figures against Nottinghamshire at Trent Bridge in a County Championship encounter. Hearne took apart the Notts first innings, taking nine for 32 from 40 overs, as the home side were bowled out for just 84.

WEDNESDAY 29th AUGUST 1900

For the first time in the club's history, six different batsmen scored half centuries in the same innings in a first-class match. It happened against Kent at Lord's as Middlesex scored 438 in reply to Kent's total of 247. Fifties from James Douglas (58), Bernard Bosanquet (51), William Robertson (52), Albert Trott (57), John Rawlin (60) and Richard Nicholls (60*) set the new club record, a feat which has only been matched twice since.

THURSDAY 29th AUGUST 1991

Mike Gatting's innings of 174 at number seven for Middlesex set a new record for an individual score by a batsman in that position in first-class matches for Middlesex, helping Middlesex to 404 against Kent at the St Lawrence Ground in Canterbury. Gatting's efforts were in vain as Middlesex went on to lose the match, being dismissed for just 96 on the final day to see Kent victorious by 208 runs.

TUESDAY 30th AUGUST 1921

The final day of the County Championship season saw Middlesex crowned champions for the second successive season. A convincing six-wicket victory over rivals Surrey rounded the season off on a high. Scoring 269 in their first innings, then bowling Middlesex out for just 132, Surrey carried a 137-run lead into the second half of the game. Five wickets from Middlesex's Nigel Haig helped dismiss Surrey for 184 in their second innings, leaving Middlesex an unlikely target of 322 for victory. Hundreds from Richard Twining (135) and Jack Hearne (106) took Middlesex to a deserved six-wicket victory and their third County Championship title.

SATURDAY 30th AUGUST 1952

Batting against Lancashire in Middlesex's final County Championship match of the 1952 season, Middlesex tail-ender and legendary bowler Alan Edward Moss rounded off a shocking season with the bat, claiming his 16th duck of the season – a club record – as he was dismissed by John Ikin without troubling the scorers again. Moss's season finished with him scoring 52 runs at an average of just 2.52, an unenviable record that will surely take a long, long time, if ever, to be surpassed.

SUNDAY 30th AUGUST 1992

Middlesex completed their final match of the 1992 Sunday League season and lifted the league title for the first and only time in the club's history. Their final opponents of the season were Surrey, who hosted the match with Middlesex at the Kennington Oval. Having only lost one Sunday League game all season, Middlesex had already been declared champions, so could afford a slip-up on the final day and still lift the trophy. In a rain-affected match Surrey posted a massive 268 for four in their 40 overs, thanks largely to a fine unbeaten 103 from Alec Stewart and 84 from Graham Thorpe. John Carr top-scored for Middlesex with 56, as they'd reached 193 for 9 after 30 overs when rain forced an early end to the match, seeing Surrey declared winners by virtue of a faster scoring rate. Middlesex, however, had the honour of lifting the trophy after a brilliant Sunday League season.

TUESDAY 31st AUGUST 1937

A memorable day for Middlesex and the end of an era, as the club's all-time leading run scorer, Patsy Hendren, played his last first-class County Championship match for the club against Surrey at Lord's. As if by destiny, Hendren signed off a truly outstanding Middlesex career with yet another hundred, his 119th for the club, scoring 103 in Middlesex's total of 419. Despite Hendren's ton, Middlesex could only achieve a draw in his final match for the county.

WEDNESDAY 31st AUGUST 1960

When Middlesex's finest wicketkeeper of all time, John Thomas (JT) Murray, caught the Worcestershire number eight batsman, Roy Booth, off the bowling of Fred Titmus on day two of a County Championship match at Lord's, it was his 99th victim of an unbelievable season. No other wicketkeeper in Middlesex history has taken more than 90 dismissals in a single season, and Murray was just one away from reaching the century. He clearly had the advantage of being behind the stumps to a fantastic Middlesex attack, including Fred Titmus, Alan Moss and Don Bennett, who supplied him with an endless string of chances behind the wicket, but this in no way should detract from Murray's club record, which is highly unlikely to ever be beaten.

MIDDLESEX CCC
On This Day

SEPTEMBER

THURSDAY 1st SEPTEMBER 1955

Legendary Middlesex bowler Frederick John (Fred) Titmus took his 158th and final first-class wicket of the 1955 season, when bowling Kent batsman Robert Wilson for 107, to set a new club record for the highest amount of first-class wickets taken in a single season by a Middlesex bowler. The record, which was set in just 27 first-class matches will in all likelihood never be broken, and surpassed the previous record of 154 which was set more than half a century earlier by Albert Trott in 1900.

SATURDAY 1st SEPTEMBER 1984

Middlesex reached their sixth one-day final in a decade as they faced Kent at Lord's in the NatWest Bank Trophy final, in a match which proved to a be a real nail-biter. Kent, captained by Chris Tavare, won the toss and chose to bat. They got off to a flying start, reaching 96 before their first wicket fell. Tavare himself, batting at three, then came to the crease and, with Chris Cowdrey and Richard Ellison, took the Kent total to a respectable 232 for six from their 60 overs. Middlesex's reply stuttered initially, reaching 88 for three in reply before Clive Radley then took control of proceedings and scored an innings of 67, a total which would quite rightly earn him the man of the match award. Needing seven runs from the last over, it came down to the scores being tied with just one ball left to face in the match. John Emburey was facing and when he turned a full-pitched delivery from Richard Ellison to square leg for a boundary, Middlesex were crowned winners of the 1984 NatWest Bank Trophy.

SUNDAY 1st SEPTEMBER 2002

Hampshire's William Kendall holds the record for the highest ever individual score by a number five batsman against Middlesex in List-A cricket, scoring 110 not out against the club at the Rose Bowl in a Norwich Union League match in 2002. Kendall's innings helped Hampshire to a total of 241 in their 45 overs, which proved to be too high for Middlesex, as they only managed to reach 217 for seven in reply, losing the match by a margin of 24 runs.

WEDNESDAY 1st SEPTEMBER 2010

Middlesex and England's Eoin Morgan put paid to rising speculation over his future at Middlesex by signing a new two-year contract with the club. Since joining the club as a 16-year-old, Morgan had rapidly grown into one of the most important players not only at Middlesex, but also within the England one-day and Twenty20 sides. Morgan stated on signing his new deal: 'I am delighted to continue my career at Middlesex. I started my association with Middlesex County Cricket Club as a 16-year-old, and the club has played a major role in me getting to where I am now. The future of the club looks very healthy and I am looking forward to playing my part when my England commitments allow."

SATURDAY 2nd SEPTEMBER 1989

Middlesex had the opportunity to defend their NatWest Bank Trophy title at Lord's against Warwickshire in 1988. Winning the toss and batting, Middlesex's innings started well, with Desmond Haynes reaching a well deserved half century. With the exception of Paul Downton's innings of 43 not out no other Middlesex batsman really got going, and a total of 210 didn't look anywhere near enough. So it proved, as Warwickshire secured the win by four wickets to ensure that Middlesex wouldn't retain the trophy. They were pushed hard by Middlesex however, reaching their target of 211 with just two balls to spare in the match.

FRIDAY 3rd SEPTEMBER 1976

After a 29-year wait, Middlesex were once again crowned County Champions, beating Surrey on the final day of the season by five wickets in a thrilling last-day finale to the season. Surrey posted 308 in their first innings, with John Edrich, cousin of Middlesex's Bill, retiring hurt having made a century. In reply, Middlesex also scored exactly 308. With the final day to play, Surrey were skittled by Middlesex inside 50 overs for 172, leaving Middlesex half of the final day to knock off the runs. Two fine innings from Middlesex batsmen took them over the line, with 67 not out from Norman Featherstone and 72 not out from Phil Edmonds, to secure a five-wicket win for Middlesex and another successful County Championship-winning season for the club.

SATURDAY 3rd SEPTEMBER 1977

Two years after losing to Lancashire, Middlesex were back again in the Gillette Cup final, this time against Glamorgan, having beaten Somerset in the semi-final. Winning the toss, Middlesex put in Glamorgan and bowled superbly to restrict them to 177 for nine in their 60 overs. Chasing, Middlesex lost captain Mike Brearley for a duck, which brought Clive Radley to the crease. He batted through the rest of the Middlesex innings and scored a match-winning 85*, as the target was reached with five wickets remaining, to secure their first ever domestic one-day trophy. Radley was the deserving man of the match.

SATURDAY 3rd SEPTEMBER 1988

Middlesex were again at Lord's in the final of the NatWest Bank Trophy to take on Worcestershire, four years after winning it against Kent. Mike Gatting won the toss and inserted Worcestershire, which was inspired, as Worcestershire lost their first three wickets for just nine runs. Phil Neale (64) and Martin Weston (31) fought back, but Worcestershire stuttered to just 161 from their 60 overs. Angus Fraser's three and Simon Hughes' four wickets did the damage for Middlesex. The Middlesex chase started badly, and when Gatting was run out first ball for 0, the score was 25 for four. This brought Mark Ramprakash (56) to the crease who, with John Emburey (36), took the total to within reach. It was left to Paul Downton to score the winning runs as Middlesex reached 162 for seven and lifted the NatWest Bank Trophy for the second time.

WEDNESDAY 4th SEPTEMBER 1901

The first 'South African' to play for Middlesex was Ernest Austin (Barberton) Halliwell in a County Championship match against Essex at Lord's, which Middlesex won by an innings and 72 runs. Halliwell represented South Africa at Test level eight times, captained them twice and was described by Wisden as the "first of the great South African wicketkeepers". Despite playing for South Africa, Halliwell was actually born in Drayton Green, Middlesex, and it was on one of his three tours to England with South Africa that he played his one and only game for the club. Halliwell was most famously known as the first wicketkeeper to place raw steaks in his keeping gloves to cushion his hands from the ball.

THURSDAY 4th SEPTEMBER 1980

Middlesex celebrated another season as County Champions with a final match away at Kent's St Lawrence Ground. Only a dogged innings of 85 not out from number eight Alan Knott dug Kent out of trouble and stopped Middlesex rounding off the season with another victory. Captain Mike Brearley scored a fine hundred (104) in Middlesex's second innings, but Middlesex had to settle for a draw. The season had seen Middlesex lose only two first-class matches all year, taking the title by 13 points ahead of Surrey, who finished in second place.

FRIDAY 5th SEPTEMBER 1969

One of the finest and most stylish modern-day batsmen to play the game, Mark Ravin Ramprakash, was born in Bushey, Hertfordshire. Having joined Middlesex as a 17-year-old, scoring 63 not out on his debut against Yorkshire, Ramprakash very quickly established himself as one of the most promising young English cricketers in the game and an essential part of the Middlesex side, captaining the club between 1997 and 1999. His Middlesex career was cut short when he crossed the river to join neighbouring Surrey in 2001, but not before he had compiled a total of 15,046 first-class runs for Middlesex at an average of 50.48. Since leaving Middlesex, Ramprakash has continued to score runs prolifically in the first-class game and is now one of only 25 players in the game's history to have amassed more than 100 hundreds in his career.

SATURDAY 6th SEPTEMBER 1975

Middlesex fans made their way to Lord's in their thousands to watch the club compete in their second one-day domestic final appearance of the season, this time in the Gillette Cup final. The opposition on the day were Lancashire who, despite great success in the competition in the early 1970s, were cast as underdogs on the day, largely as a result of Middlesex technically benefitting from 'home advantage'. Disappointingly for the massed Middlesex fans, a certain West Indian by the name of Clive Hubert Lloyd turned up at the Home of Cricket with other ideas, and blasted his way to a match-winning score of 73 not out to take Lancashire past the Middlesex target of 180 and secure a seven-wicket victory.

SATURDAY 6th SEPTEMBER 1980

Five years after losing the Gillette Cup final on exactly the same day, Middlesex were back at Lord's in the final, this time against London rivals, Surrey. Losing the toss, Surrey were put in to bat by Middlesex captain, Mike Brearley, and they proceeded to post a total of 201 in their 60 overs, with David Smith top-scoring for Surrey with 50. In Middlesex's reply Mike Brearley led from the front with a brilliant 96 not out, opening the batting, to take them to their target with Roland Butcher, who finished on an unbeaten half century. Middlesex won by seven wickets with more than six overs to spare to lift the crown for the second time in their history.

WEDNESDAY 7th SEPTEMBER 1977

A thrilling end to the 1977 season saw Gloucestershire leading the table on 216 points with one game to go, with Kent and Middlesex jointly in second place on 211 points. Middlesex faced Lancashire at Stanley Park, Blackpool, Kent travelled to Edgbaston to play Warwickshire and Gloucestershire took on Hampshire at Bristol. With Gloucestershire capitulating, losing heavily to Hampshire, and Kent winning narrowly by 27 runs, it was left to Middlesex to secure 17 points or more to win the title. They could only match Kent's effort and while winning as Phil Edmonds and John Emburey picked up 17 of the Lancashire wickets, they only secured 16 points. For the second time in the club's history, they had to share the County Championship trophy.

THURSDAY 8th SEPTEMBER 1994

Middlesex batsman John Donald Carr batted through to the close of the opening day to score the highest individual first-class score by a Middlesex player batting at number five, scoring 261 not out against Gloucestershire at Lord's. His magnificent innings came in a Middlesex first-innings total of 513 in a game they won comfortably by an innings and 63 runs, having dismissed Gloucestershire for 199 and 251. Carr's innings also broke a second club record on the day, that of the highest ever first-class sixth wicket partnership, when he and Paul Weekes put on a 270 partnership which only came to an end when Weekes was caught by Courtenay Walsh off the bowling of Martyn Ball for 94.

FRIDAY 9th SEPTEMBER 2005

In what has been billed as the greatest Ashes Test series of all time, England went into the final match of the 2005 series at the Brit Oval, Kennington, needing a draw to win back the Ashes, ending an Australian dominance that had spanned 16 years and eight series wins. Day two of the match saw the England first innings come to a close with 373 runs on the board, with Middlesex's Andrew Strauss instrumental in the total, scoring an amazing 129 runs before eventually falling to Aussie legend Shane Warne. Strauss's innings, when England wickets were falling around him, set up a sizeable enough first-innings total to put England in control of the game and successfully gain the draw they needed from the final match of the series to secure an historic Ashes win for England.

WEDNESDAY 10th SEPTEMBER 1986

One of the hottest modern-day talents in world cricket, Middlesex and England's Eoin Joseph Gerard Morgan, was born in Dublin, Ireland. Morgan, who made his first-class Middlesex debut in 2006, already has more than 4,000 runs to his name for Middlesex in all forms of the game, including four first-class hundreds and three List-A hundreds. He has represented England at Test level on six occasions, already has a Test hundred under his belt after scoring 130 against Pakistan at Trent Bridge in 2010, and has also scored three One-Day International hundreds for England in the 39 ODIs he has played in, at the time of writing.

MONDAY 10th SEPTEMBER 2007

History was made as Lord's hosted its first ever floodlit cricket match, as Middlesex took on the Derbyshire Phantoms under the lights and in front of the live Sky television cameras. Middlesex rose to the occasion and comfortably beat Derbyshire in the NatWest Pro40 League match by a margin of four wickets. With the popularity of day/night cricket taking off around the world, Marylebone Cricket Club agreed to install temporary floodlights for the match in a trial at the Home of Cricket, which ultimately proved successful and led to the installation of four new state-of-the-art, bespoke designed, permanent telescopic floodlights at Lord's in 2009.

MONDAY 11th SEPTEMBER 1995

A brilliant match at Park Road, Uxbridge saw Middlesex beat Leicestershire by the narrowest of margins of just one run in this thrilling first-class County Championship encounter. Having dismissed Middlesex for 338 in their first innings, Leicestershire then scored 300 in theirs. Middlesex's second innings was declared on just 212 for two, leaving Leicestershire needing just 251 runs to secure victory in the fourth innings. At 131 for three, Leicestershire looked to be cruising until the spin of Phil Tufnell (5-100) and John Emburey (4-81) regained the momentum for Middlesex, with the final Leicestershire wicket falling with the score on 249, agonisingly short of the winning post.

THURSDAY 12th SEPTEMBER 1996

The record for the most first-class runs scored by a batsman in a match is held jointly by two batsmen, one of which is Paul Nicholas Weekes, who in a match starting on this day scored an aggregate of 331 runs for Middlesex in a drawn County Championship match against Somerset at Park Road, Uxbridge. His first-innings total of 171 not out in a total of 350 was backed up with a brilliant 160 in the second-innings total of 357. The other batsman to hold this record is John DB (Jack) Robertson, who amazingly managed the feat in just one innings, as he wasn't required to bat in a Middlesex second innings.

TUESDAY 13th SEPTEMBER 1932

Amazingly, it was as a fresh faced 13-year-old schoolboy that legendary Middlesex batsman, Denis Charles Scott Compton, scored his first hundred at Lord's, not playing for Middlesex, but for a London Elementary Schools XI in a one-day match against CF Tufnell's Public Schools XI. Opening the batting for the Elementary Schools, Compton scored a faultless and match-winning 114 in a total of 204, before also taking two wickets for just five runs in four overs as Tufnell's side were dismissed for just 56 to see Compton's side win by a convincing 148 runs. Middlesex legend Pelham 'Plum' Warner, who was at Lord's watching the game, was so impressed with Compton that he offered him a role on the MCC groundstaff immediately. The rest, as they say, is history.

MONDAY 13th SEPTEMBER 2010

Middlesex announced the signing of West Indies paceman Corey Collymore from Sussex on a two-year contract. Collymore joined Middlesex after a successful spell with Sussex, helping them to achieve promotion to the first division of the County Championship in 2010. In 2010 Collymore took 57 first-class wickets for Sussex at an average of just 19.87 and 33 wickets at 33.34 in 2009. On signing Collymore, Middlesex's managing director of cricket Angus Fraser said: "Signing Corey is a major coup for Middlesex CCC. He will add quality and control to our attack. His figures in all forms of the game tell you how good a bowler he is and he comes with a very good reputation for helping and working with other younger bowlers."

MONDAY 14th SEPTEMBER 1903

Crowned first-class County Championship winners for the first time in their history after losing just one match all season, Middlesex earned the right to play as the Champion County against The Rest at the Kennington Oval. Batting first, Middlesex posted a total of 230, with George Beldam and Bernard Bosanquet scoring 57 and 58 respectively. Middlesex then dismissed The Rest for just 184, with Jack Hearne and Albert Trott taking three wickets apiece. Pelham 'Plum' Warner's brilliant hundred (115) and another fine innings of 88 from Beldam helped Middlesex to a total of 254, leaving The Rest needing 301 for victory. They reached 229 for five at stumps on the final day of the match, which finished in a draw.

TUESDAY 14th SEPTEMBER 1982

Middlesex completed their final County Championship match of the season with a ten-wicket victory over Worcestershire at New Road, Worcester, and celebrated winning the County Championship title once again – for the ninth time. A brilliant season, in which Middlesex only lost two County Championship fixtures all year, saw them finish 39 points clear of their nearest rivals Leicestershire. This Championship win can really be put down to a great team effort, as three separate Middlesex bowlers took more than 70 first-class wickets in the Championship – Edmonds (71), Emburey (74) and Daniel (71). Four separate batsmen each scored more than 1,000 runs in the Championship – Brearley (1,023), Butcher (1,013), Gatting (1,273) and Slack (1,109).

WEDNESDAY 15th SEPTEMBER 1920

Middlesex celebrated their second County Championship-winning season with the Champion County fixture against The Rest at the Kennington Oval. It was a batsman from The Rest who shone in this three-day fixture, however, as Surrey legend Jack Berry Hobbs scored a magnificent double hundred in The Rest's first innings. His 215 helped The Rest's total to 603 for five declared in reply to Middlesex's first-innings total of 318 all out. Middlesex reached 192 for four at the close on the final day to earn a draw. Patsy Hendren rounded off a great season for Middlesex, in which he scored more than 2,500 runs at an average of 61.46, by scoring 65 and 67 in the two Middlesex innings.

THURSDAY 15th SEPTEMBER 1921

Having successfully defended their County Championship title and lost only three first-class matches all season, Middlesex found The Rest too strong in the County Champions match at the Oval, losing the game by nine wickets and suffering their heaviest defeat of the year. Middlesex were bowled out for 220 in their first innings, with The Rest making 345. Middlesex's second innings reached only 160, leaving The Rest needing just 36 runs to win the match.

MONDAY 15th SEPTEMBER 1947

The final match of the 1947 season brought to an end one of the most amazing seasons in the club's history. The double act of Denis Compton and Bill Edrich signed off a sun baked summer with a fitting performance in the final first-class match of the season against The Rest. It put the icing on the season of all seasons for the pair and was a fine tribute to Middlesex's fourth County Championship-winning season. Compton made a sublime 246 in Middlesex's first innings – and Edrich an equally magnificent 180 – to help Middlesex to their highest ever total against The Rest in the County Championship finale to the season. Compton had scored 2,467 first-class runs at an average of 102.79, including a club record 13 centuries for Middlesex, whilst Edrich had scored 2,650 first-class runs at 85.48. Edrich's feat of scoring more than 2,500 first-class runs in a season has only been matched by two other batsmen in the entire history of the club.

SATURDAY 16th SEPTEMBER 1990

Middlesex reached their first and only one-day 40-over final in the short-lived Refuge Assurance Cup, as a result of finishing third and defeating Lancashire by 45 runs in the semi-final play off. Derbyshire were crowned champions of the Refuge Assurance League and defeated Nottinghamshire in their semi-final to earn their place in the final against Middlesex, played at Edgbaston. Under the brilliant one-day captaincy of Mike Gatting, Middlesex won the toss and elected to field. Derbyshire's Kim Barnett scored a quickfire 42 and Johnny Morris a solid 46, leading to a total for Derbyshire of 197 for seven in their 40 overs. In the Middlesex chase, Desmond Haynes, Mike Gatting and Keith Brown all reached the 40s, but it was left to Paul Downton to score an unbeaten 34 to win the trophy for Middlesex in the final over of the match.

THURSDAY 16th SEPTEMBER 1993

Having been through the entire County Championship season unbeaten, Middlesex had the County Championship already wrapped up and in their hands when they travelled to New Road, Worcester, for the final match of the season. You could possibly therefore excuse some complacency from Middlesex, as runners-up Worcestershire cruised to victory by an innings and 36 runs. Middlesex's first innings yielded just 68 runs, and their second only produced 148. Despite only managing 252 themselves in their innings, it was enough to secure an innings victory for Worcestershire.

TUESDAY 17th SEPTEMBER 1985

The final day of the 1985 season saw Middlesex again crowned winners of the County Championship after completing a brilliant season with a dominant win over Warwickshire by an innings and 74 runs at Edgbaston. Needing to win to secure the title, Middlesex went about their business as they had done all year, by bowling out the home side for just 187, before amassing a huge 445 in reply. Needing 259 to make Middlesex even bat again, Warwickshire were dismissed for just 184 to suffer a huge defeat and see Middlesex crowned county champions again. Considering Middlesex won the title so convincingly, by a margin of 36 points, it was surprising that not one single Middlesex batsman made more than 1,000 runs in the County Championship season.

FRIDAY 18th SEPTEMBER 2009

Sat precariously at the bottom of the table, Middlesex went into the final day of their County Championship season at Uxbridge looking to firstly avoid losing to Derbyshire and secondly to dodge winning the wooden spoon, something they had never suffered in their entire history. Also at the bottom of the table with Middlesex were Surrey and Leicestershire. On the final day and batting for the draw, Middlesex's Adam London, at number seven with a broken finger, scored a brilliant and match-saving innings of 65. When he fell, Middlesex's bowlers Tim Murtagh and David Burton survived the final three overs to cling on for the draw. Surrey duly drew with Glamorgan, and Leicestershire were trounced by Northamptonshire to leave the Grace Road side with the wooden spoon. Middlesex finished just two points ahead of them in the table.

WEDNESDAY 19th SEPTEMBER 2007

Middlesex went into their final match of the County Championship season knowing that two things were required for them to achieve immediate promotion back into the first division, having been relegated in 2006. Firstly, Middlesex had to go to Chelmsford and win heavily against Essex; then Nottinghamshire, just above Middlesex in the table, had to lose heavily and gain no points from the game. Sadly neither happened, as Middlesex were annihilated by Essex, going down by ten wickets, and Notts picked up the point they needed to secure their promotion. Middlesex were therefore condemned to a second season in the second division. Middlesex took something from the game, however – the emergence of a young and rapid pace bowler on debut, called Robbie Williams, who took five for 112 in the Essex first innings.

THURSDAY 20th SEPTEMBER 1990

The final day of the 1990 season once again saw Middlesex crowned county champions – their sixth title in under 15 years. A final match of the season away at Hove against Sussex saw Middlesex win convincingly, by an innings and 57 runs. Middlesex posted a healthy 411 all out. Despite a magnificent 116 not out from Keith Brown, Sussex struggled to come to terms with the Middlesex bowling attack and were rolled over for 187 in their first innings and just 167 in their second.

THURSDAY 21st SEPTEMBER 2006

Middlesex bowler Chris Peploe will choose to forget this County Championship match against Kent, as the completion of his 50th over saw him become the most expensive Middlesex bowler ever in a match. The 205th run scored off his bowling saw him break a 100-year-old club record, but despite his record breaking figures Middlesex managed to bravely hang on for a draw in the game, having been forced to follow on.

FRIDAY 22nd SEPTEMBER 1978

In Dublin, Ireland, Edmund Christopher (Ed) Joyce, one of Ireland's greatest cricketers, was born. Joyce made his debut for Middlesex in 1999, and spent nine years with Middlesex before leaving to join Sussex. Joyce quickly established himself as a regular within the Middlesex side with his commanding batting style. In the absence of injured captain Ed Smith, Joyce captained the side in the club's successful 2008 Twenty20 Cup campaign, and was skipper on finals day as Middlesex lifted their first silverware for 15 years. Joyce scored an impressive 8,278 first-class runs at an average of 46.76 in his 118 first-class matches for Middlesex and also knocked up 3,235 List-A runs at 32.02 in 124 appearances.

WEDNESDAY 22nd SEPTEMBER 2010

Adam Gilchrist was named as the winner of the 2010 Walter Lawrence Trophy, the award given to the batsman who has scored the fastest century in the domestic cricket season. Gilchrist won the trophy for his brilliant 47-ball hundred against the Kent Spitfires, when playing for Middlesex at Canterbury on June 11th.

SATURDAY 23rd SEPTEMBER 2006

A dismal season for Middlesex came to an end with the side suffering relegation to the second division of the County Championship for the first time since two leagues were introduced. Only one Championship win all season, with eight draws and seven losses, was the kind of form that saw Middlesex finish rock bottom and drop to the second division. The final match of the season, against Kent at the St Lawrence Ground, finished with Middlesex claiming a draw after Kent had outplayed them, amassing a huge total of 603 for six declared in their first innings. Middlesex also suffered relegation in the NatWest Pro40 this season.

SUNDAY 23rd SEPTEMBER 2007

In stark contrast to a year earlier, Middlesex were celebrating on the final day of the 2007 season in front of the live Sky TV cameras, as a NatWest Pro40 play-off match victory over Northamptonshire saw the club bounce straight back into the top flight of the competition. Northamptonshire were dismissed for just 148, leaving Middlesex with a moderate target to reach to secure promotion. An 18-year-old pace bowler, Steven Finn, stole the show, taking three for 30 from his eight overs. In reply Middlesex reached their target easily to secure a six-wicket victory and celebrate promotion.

SATURDAY 24th SEPTEMBER 2005

The final day of the 2005 County Championship season saw Middlesex lose heavily to Surrey by an innings and 39 runs at the Kennington Oval, yet despite this it was the Middlesex team who were celebrating. Middlesex and Surrey sat right at the foot of the division one table, with both sides looking to avoid the drop. Runs were crucial to Middlesex, and when captain Ben Hutton won the toss he batted. Middlesex put on 404 for five and declared with maximum batting points. This left Middlesex needing just one bowling point from the game to survive and send their rivals down. The crucial wicket and bowling point came on the second day and Middlesex stayed up. Surrey went on to pile on a huge yet somewhat irrelevant 686 for five before declaring and dismissing Middlesex for 243 in their second innings, securing a massive yet largely hollow victory.

FRIDAY 25th SEPTEMBER 1987

At a meeting held at Lord's by the club's committee, the agenda included whether to offer two 'young and promising prospects' professional contracts with the club. After some deliberation, it was agreed that two-year contracts would be offered to both Paul Nicholas Weekes and Mark Ravin Ramprakash, as they were both considered to be 'ones for the future'. Meetings were arranged with the players and their parents, and contracts were duly agreed and signed. Both went on to have fine careers with the club, with Weekes making 233 first-class appearances and scoring just short of 11,000 runs, while Ramprakash made 211 appearances and scored more than 15,000 runs.

TUESDAY 26th SEPTEMBER 2006

Following a truly shocking season which saw Middlesex relegated from the top flight of the County Championship and also relegated to the second division of the NatWest Pro40 competition, Middlesex did win some silverware at the Professional Cricketers' Association awards, as the club were awarded the 'MCC Spirit of Cricket County Team Award'. The annual award is presented to the most disciplined county side in the three domestic competitions. Not surprisingly, the award came as little comfort to the club and its fans.

WEDNESDAY 27th SEPTEMBER 2006

Following a year of team performances which must rank as one of the worst in the club's history, Middlesex captain Ben Hutton resigned the captaincy of the club, citing ill health, loss of form and the weight of captaincy bearing down on him as the reasons for his resignation. Middlesex's chief executive Vinny Codrington said: "Ben is committed, passionate and caring, and this selfless act is a typical gesture on behalf of the club. Everybody involved with Middlesex will be thrilled as soon as he gets his next hundred." Rather ironically, Hutton did just this in his next match for the club, scoring 118 in the opening match of the 2007 season.

SATURDAY 27th SEPTEMBER 2008

As the 2008 season neared its end, Middlesex were chasing promotion to the top flight of the County Championship structure, but they had to settle for finishing third and missed out on promotion for the second year in a row by just one place. A strong finish to the season proved to be to no avail, as it merely took Middlesex to within touching distance of promotion. They followed up a brilliant eight-wicket win over second-placed Worcestershire at Kidderminster in their penultimate match, with a convincing 93-run victory over Northamptonshire at the County Ground, where Andrew Strauss (172), Owais Shah (114) and Eoin Morgan (136*) each made centuries in Middlesex's first innings of 545 for seven declared. Northants were bowled out for 256 before Middlesex declared on 171 for two in their second innings. Shaun Udal followed up his five for 69 in the first innings, with three for 96 in the second, as Northants were bowled out for 367.

SUNDAY 28th SEPTEMBER 1975

Test-playing Australian pace bowler Stuart Rupert Clark was born in Sutherland, New South Wales. Clark joined Middlesex as the club's overseas player for the 2004 and 2005 seasons, but was restricted by injury to just seven first-class matches for Middlesex in his time at the club. Clark scored 34 on debut in August of 2004 against Northamptonshire and took two for 47 with the ball. In total he scored 116 runs at an average of 16.57 for Middlesex and took 25 wickets at 25.61, with best bowling figures of five for 61. Middlesex undoubtedly didn't see the best of a very talented Australian cricketer in the time he spent with the club at Lord's.

TUESDAY 29th SEPTEMBER 1992

Having first been proposed by the TCCB the previous year for consideration, the issue of players' coloured clothing was again brought onto the agenda of a Middlesex general committee meeting at Lord's. With directives from the TCCB informing first-class counties that coloured clothing was to be introduced into one-day domestic cricket, the club's committee voted on which of the four proposed designs and colour schemes would be most appropriate for Middlesex to play in. Whilst the overall consensus was that no one was in agreement of the introduction of 'pyjama cricket', as it was being called, it was reluctantly agreed that if anything were to be selected then the 'least garish' of the four designs would be adopted by the club, and that the chosen colours were 'dark' and 'the palest blue'.

MONDAY 30th SEPTEMBER 1991

At a Middlesex CCC general committee, 'Benefit Middlesex 92' was agreed upon and launched to raise revenue for the development of youth cricket within Middlesex. Benefit Middlesex 92 was launched to the club's membership with its own benefit brochure, which included full details of the programme that lay ahead throughout 1992, and was launched in the absence of any players' benefit season that year. A number of high profile fund-raising dinners, cricket and golf days and members' functions, with much involvement from the playing staff and the serving committee, ensured that the scheme was a huge success for the club and was well supported by its members.

MIDDLESEX CCC
On This Day

OCTOBER

MONDAY 1st OCTOBER 2007

Having resigned the captaincy at the end of the previous season, Ben Hutton, grandson of the legendary Len, announced his retirement from professional cricket. Hutton retired at the age of just 30, having played 108 first-class matches, scoring 5,712 runs for the club at an average of 33.60. Middlesex stalwart Richard Leonard Johnson also retired from playing, having played 93 first-class matches for the club, scoring 1,731 runs at 14.92 and taking 279 wickets at 28.46. Johnson was to return to Middlesex in the 2010 season as assistant coach, working alongside Richard Scott, Middlesex's head coach.

THURSDAY 2nd OCTOBER 1873

Pelham Francis (Plum) Warner, or the 'Grand old man of English cricket' as he was known, was born in Port-of-Spain, Trinidad. Warner sits just outside the top ten of all time first-class run scorers for Middlesex, having scored 19,507 for the club at an average of 37.44 in a career between 1894 and 1920. Warner captained Middlesex for more than a decade, leading the team to the County Championship crown in 1920, and has a stand named after him at Lord's Cricket Ground. Warner captained England on the successful Ashes tour of 1903/1904, securing a 3-2 series win over Australia to retain the Ashes. After retiring he became the team manager of England, leading them to Australia for the infamous Bodyline series in 1932/33. He was honoured with an MBE in 1937 for his services to the game.

WEDNESDAY 3rd OCTOBER 2001

Both Mark Ramprakash and Owais Shah were Middlesex's representatives in the England side which toured Zimbabwe in the winter of 2001, playing a key role in England's 5-0 whitewash over the Zimbabwean's in the One-Day International series. The series began with the first ODI on this day, played at the Harare Sports Club, and surprisingly it was Ramprakash's efforts with the ball which outshone his batting. Zimbabwe were dismissed inside their 50 overs for 206, with England's current team director, Andy Flower, top-scoring for the home side with 59. Ramprakash returned figures of three for 28 and made a useful 35 in England's reply, as they cruised home by five wickets with more than three overs to spare.

FRIDAY 4th OCTOBER 1957

One of the most highly decorated military officers ever to play for Middlesex died on this day, aged 72. Clarence Napier Bruce, 3rd Baron Aberdare, played for the club in 62 first-class matches between 1908 and 1929, scoring just short of 3,000 runs. His highest score was 149 against Lancashire in 1919. Napier entered the British Army at the outbreak of World War One, and lost his elder brother in the war in 1914. Among others, he served with the Glamorgan Yeomanry, Guards Machine Gun Regiment and reached the rank of captain. He served as an honorary colonel in the Welsh Heavy AA Brigade and as an acting major in the Surrey Home Guards during World War Two. In 1949 he received a CBE and was made a Knight Grand Cross of the British Empire in 1954. He died in a motoring accident, when his vehicle crashed and fell into a river bed in Yugoslavia.

SUNDAY 5th OCTOBER 1873

Herbert Bailey Hayman, a hard-hitting opening batsman who played for Middlesex between 1893 and 1901, was born in Willesden, Middlesex. Hayman made 86 first-class appearances for Middlesex scoring more than 3,500 runs in his 154 innings. In May 1896 he enjoyed an opening partnership of 218 with the great Andrew Stoddart at Lord's against Yorkshire, scoring 152 runs himself, and then in 1901 he was again involved in a double hundred opening partnership – this time of 200 – with the legendary Pelham Warner, when he scored 110 runs. His highest individual innings of 165 came when playing for AJ Webbe's XI, also of Middlesex legendary status, against Oxford University in 1901.

SATURDAY 6th OCTOBER 1917

The longest-serving official scorer in the club's history, Harry Sharp, was born on this day in Kentish Town, London. Sharp joined Middlesex in rather fortuitous circumstances, as he had been spotted by Middlesex's Jack Durston while practising in the Middlesex Indoor School in Acton. He made his debut in 1946 and played until 1955, making 162 appearances and scoring 6,141 runs at 25.80, including nine hundreds and 30 half centuries. In 1973 Sharp took on the club's official scoring duties, holding the post for 20 years until his retirement at the age of 75 in 1993.

TUESDAY 7th OCTOBER 1997

Work was completed on the newly refurbished Middlesex Academy in Finchley, previously known simply as "the cricket and squash centre". After a major investment the centre was ready for re-opening, rebranded as the Middlesex Sports Academy. The new facility offered the very latest fitness facilities, a gymnasium and sports hall complete with new cricket net lanes and refurbished squash courts. The academy also offered conference and meeting facilities, a bar, catering and a sports shop selling cricket equipment and Middlesex merchandise.

MONDAY 8th OCTOBER 1990

Having been the club's principal sponsor for the previous three years, Nixdorf Computer were acquired by the global Scandinavian technology giant, Siemens, which threw some doubt over their continued commitment to the club. An interim sponsorship agreement of one year was agreed, and for the 1990 season alone, Middlesex's principal sponsor became 'Siemens Nixdorf Information Systems'.

FRIDAY 9th OCTOBER 1987

Middlesex captain Mike Gatting led England as captain to the fourth One-Day World Cup, played in India and Pakistan. Gatting's side opened their campaign with a nail-biting victory over the fancied West Indians by two wickets in Gujranwala. Gatting's side included Middlesex men Paul Downton and John Emburey, who both played in the opening match. England needed 244 for victory and reached their target in the final over, with just three balls to spare. England were grouped with Pakistan and Sri Lanka in group B, and finished second behind Pakistan, with a record of played six, won four, lost two.

WEDNESDAY 10th OCTOBER 2007

Owais Shah was the sole Middlesex representative in the England side to play the One-Day International series in Sri Lanka in 2007/08. England went into the penultimate match in Colombo 2-1 up in the series, knowing that victory would give them an unassailable lead. Shah had hit a magnificent 82 off 92 balls in the second ODI to earn himself the man of the match award, but only managed nine runs in this match before having his stumps uprooted by Lasith Malinga. Despite this, England successfully chased down Sri Lanka's total of 211 to win the series.

TUESDAY 11th OCTOBER 2005

A few eyebrows were raised when Middlesex announced the signing of one of the most famous and well known sportsmen in living memory, Mohammed Ali. Upon further investigation however it became apparent that it wasn't the boxer, but the former Derbyshire pace bowler who had signed for the club. Unlike his boxing namesake, the cricketing Mohammed Ali proved to be less of knockout, as he went on to only make five first-class appearances for the club, taking just ten first-class wickets at an average of 45.30.

FRIDAY 12th OCTOBER 2007

Despite initially receiving a slightly mixed reaction from many Middlesex supporters earlier in the season, the club's newly designed pink Twenty20 playing kit, launched in celebration of Middlesex's charity partnership with Breakthrough Breast Cancer, was honoured with an award for innovation from the ECB at their Annual First Class County Marketing Awards night. The club had raised more than £20,000 for the charity during the season, largely from replica shirt sales, which was no doubt a major factor in the ECB awarding the trophy to Middlesex.

SATURDAY 13th OCTOBER 1877

Bernard James Tindal Bosanquet was born in Enfield, Middlesex. Bosanquet played for Middlesex between 1899 and 1919. He was considered a very good all-rounder, who was well capable of scoring runs on his day, and was a tidy medium-fast bowler in his earlier career. It was when away at Oxford University that he achieved infamy for his most notorious moment, as Bosanquet is credited with creating the 'googly' delivery. Apparently he created and practiced the delivery during a university game called 'Twisty-Twosty', where you had to pitch the ball on a table and bounce it in a fashion where your opponent was unable to catch it. He refined the delivery in the game so that he could pitch the ball and make it turn to the right or left, with little change to his delivery action. He then brought this technique to the cricket field to great effect, and the googly was born. Bosanquet took 134 wickets in the 1904 season, leading to an England call-up where he used the googly extensively, taking eight for 107 in the opening Test match of the 1905 Ashes series at Trent Bridge.

MONDAY 14th OCTOBER 1912

John Albert (Jack) Young, the sixth-highest first-class wicket taker in Middlesex's history, was born in Paddington, London. A slow left-arm orthodox bowler, Young took 1,182 wickets at an average of 19.21 in a Middlesex career between 1933 and 1956 and was an integral part of the club's championship-winning sides of 1947 and 1949. His career best bowling figures for Middlesex were 8-31 and he made eight Test appearances for England, taking 17 wickets at 44.52.

THURSDAY 15th OCTOBER 2009

After a special general meeting, Middlesex County Cricket Club announced the results of the election ballot for the club's new executive board to replace the existing general committee. There were a total of 2,539 votes cast from within the membership, with Chris Lowe, Paul Downton, Don Bennett, Alan Moss, David Kendix and Chris Goldie receiving the most votes and duly being elected onto the new Middlesex CCC executive board. They joined chairman Ian Lovett, chief executive Vinny Codrington, head of finance Richard Goatley, managing director of cricket Angus Fraser and treasurer Geoff Norris.

FRIDAY 15th OCTOBER 2010

Middlesex's Shaun Udal announced his retirement from professional cricket. Udal had joined Middlesex in 2008 and was a key part of the team that won the Twenty20 Cup that season, with the spin partnership he formed with Murali Kartik being the deciding factor in many of Middlesex's victories in the cup run. Udal played in 41 first-class matches for Middlesex and took 98 wickets at an average of 31.08, with personal best bowling figures of six for 36 coming against Surrey at the Brit Oval in 2009.

THURSDAY 16th OCTOBER 1975

One of the finest all rounders that South African cricket has ever produced, Jacques Henry Kallis, was born in Pinelands, Cape Town, South Africa. Kallis represented Middlesex as the club's overseas player in the 1997 season, playing 16 first-class matches and scoring 1,034 runs in the season at an average of 47.00, as well as taking 32 wickets at an average of 20.46. In List-A matches he scored 338 runs at 22.53 and took 12 wickets at 25.83.

TUESDAY 17th OCTOBER 1967

In Edgware, Middlesex, Alistair Gregory James Foster, the younger brother of Angus, was born. Alistair, like his brother, played first-class cricket for Middlesex, however never quite achieved the same level of success as his brother, despite showing huge promise at the outset of his Middlesex career. He made his first-class debut for Middlesex in June of 1986 against the touring New Zealanders at Lord's and took three for 46 in the Kiwis' second innings when opening the bowling with Norman Cowans. Fraser left Middlesex to join Essex in 1991 having been unable to secure a regular spot in Middlesex's first XI. He played his final first-class match in 1992 for Essex and, after a lengthy absence from the professional game, returned to Middlesex for a second spell in the 1998 season, when he played 11 matches as a one day specialist in List-A matches only.

FRIDAY 17th OCTOBER 2008

Middlesex announced that after qualifying for the forthcoming Stanford Super Series, Marston's, the official beer brewer for the England cricket team, had agreed to become the club's shirt sponsor throughout the course of the forthcoming tournament in Antigua. Middlesex played in each of their Stanford Super Series matches with specially printed pink shirts, emblazoned with the Marston's Pedigree logo across the front. The club ordered a short run of replica 'Marston's Stanford shirts' to sell in the club shop at Lord's, which sold out quickly and have become something of a collectors' item ever since.

WEDNESDAY 18th OCTOBER 2006

Following a season of relegation from the top flight of the County Championship and the NatWest Pro40, Middlesex signalled their intentions to bounce back at the first attempt by announcing the signings of overseas stars Chaminda Vaas and Murali Kartik. Vaas, a hugely experienced Sri Lankan pace bowler, and Kartik, a world class left-arm spinner from India, were seen as the perfect duo to take Middlesex straight back into division one in both major domestic competitions – sadly for the club they failed to achieve promotion in the County Championship, but courtesy of a last day victory in a promotion play-off match with Northamptonshire they were successfully promoted into the first division of the NatWest Pro40.

TUESDAY 19th OCTOBER 1993

The on-field rivalry between Middlesex and Surrey is both long standing and widely acknowledged by fans and members of the two clubs. In 1993 the rivalry spilled off the field, with the two counties reaching loggerheads over the matter of who technically 'owned' the borough of Spelthorne. Spelthorne sits across the border of both counties and contains towns with the postal districts of both Middlesex and Surrey. A representative of the Middlesex committee reported back to the club on this day that meetings with Surrey CCC had not proved 'fruitful' and that both parties had 'unreservedly agreed to disagree'. At the heart of the dispute were a number of promising young cricketers within the Spelthorne area who had signed up to play for Middlesex Young Cricketers as opposed to Surrey, much to the latter's obvious annoyance.

TUESDAY 20th OCTOBER 1987

Middlesex and England off-spinner John Emburey ended any speculation about his future playing career by signing a new three-year contract with Middlesex. Emburey had originally declined the opportunity to sign a new contract extension offered by Middlesex, entering into talks with Warwickshire CCC instead. Emburey was keen to fulfil his ambition of captaining a first-class county, and his opportunities with Middlesex were limited given the club's success under Mike Gatting. Having already released Phil Edmonds from his Middlesex contract that year due to continued complications over his off-field business interests, Middlesex faced life in 1988 without either of their legendary 'spin twins', so Emburey's decision to sign a new offer and remain with the club came as a great relief to all at Lord's. With 13 years at Middlesex already under his belt, Emburey remained at the club for a further eight years before eventually leaving at the end of the 1995 season.

WEDNESDAY 20th OCTOBER 2005

Middlesex announced that Jamie Dalrymple had accepted the terms of a new deal with the club and had signed a new contract which would see him remain at Middlesex until the end of the 2007 season. Dalrymple had made his first-class debut for Middlesex as a 20-year-old in 2001, and was to leave Middlesex at the completion of this contract, moving to Glamorgan to take the role of captain.

SATURDAY 21st OCTOBER 1961

England weren't to experience a tour to Pakistan until 1961 when, under the leadership of Ted Dexter, they played a three-match Test series starting on this day with the opening match in the Gaddafi Stadium, Lahore. Middlesex's Eric Russell and John (JT) Murray were in the England side, and both players did the club proud in the opening Test, as Murray claimed six dismissals behind the stumps in the match and Russell scored 34 in the England first innings. England comfortably won the opening match by five wickets and drew the remaining two Tests to claim a 1-0 series win. Despite missing out on the first Test, Middlesex's Peter Parfitt also toured with the party. He played in the second and third Tests, scoring a century (111) in the third and final match in Karachi.

SUNDAY 22nd OCTOBER 1978

Owais Alam Shah, the fifth-highest List-A run scorer in the club's history and the only Middlesex batsman to score 12 List-A centuries for the club, was born in Karachi, Pakistan. Shah scored a total of 7,092 List-A runs for the club at an average of 36.36, including a club record 12 centuries and 45 half centuries in a Middlesex career spanning 1995 to 2010. Shah also achieved six Test caps for England, 71 One-Day International caps and 17 International Twenty20 caps.

THURSDAY 23rd OCTOBER 2008

With success in the 2008 Twenty20 Cup campaign came the reward of representing England in the Champions League T20. The draw for the 2008 competition was made on this day, with Middlesex being drawn against the Victoria Bushrangers, who had won the Australian domestic T20 competition, the Chennai Super Kings, who finished as runners-up in the previous Indian Premier League, and the Pretoria Titans, winners of South Africa's own domestic Twenty20 competition, with Middlesex scheduled to kick off the tournament in the opening game in Mumbai against Victoria on 3rd December. The other group included the Rajasthan Royals of India, the Sialkot Stallions of Pakistan, the Western Warriors of Australia and the Natal Dolphins of South Africa. Little were Middlesex to know at this point that the competition would not even take place, as events unfolded in the coming weeks.

FRIDAY 24th OCTOBER 2008

Middlesex CCC announced that they would be appointing Angus Fraser to the staff as the club's new managing director of cricket. It was felt that the time had come for the club to have someone in a position of seniority to oversee the business of cricket, from grass roots to professional level in Middlesex. In what can only be described as a broad role, Fraser's remit was, among other things, to ensure the general well being of cricket across the county at all levels. As a player who had himself progressed through the ranks from the Middlesex League with Stanmore to representing Middlesex at first-class level and England at Test and ODI level, Fraser himself was the perfect blueprint for what the club hoped could be achieved with much greater frequency.

SATURDAY 25th OCTOBER 2008

Shaun Udal was named as Middlesex's captain for the club's 2008 winter close-season competitions, including the forthcoming inaugural Stanford Super Series, the Champions League T20 competitions and the 2009 season. Udal had joined Middlesex at the start of the 2008 campaign, having left Hampshire after 18 years. He stated upon being appointed as captain: "It is an unbelievable honour to captain this great and proud club, and it is my intention to return it to its glory days of years gone by." A little known fact is that Shaun's grandfather played for Middlesex in those years gone by he referred to, albeit very briefly, as Geoffrey Francis Uvedale Udal made just one appearance for the club in 1932 at Lord's against Yorkshire.

SUNDAY 25th OCTOBER 2009

Nick Compton, grandson of the legendary Denis Compton, informed the club that he wished to accept an offer from Somerset County Cricket Club, and left Middlesex to join the Taunton-based side. Compton had been with Middlesex for six seasons, and felt that he needed a new challenge in his cricketing career. On leaving the club, Compton said: "Having the opportunity to play for Middlesex at Lord's, to follow in the footsteps of not only my grandfather but many great past players, makes me very proud and also respectful of my place in a long line of history at Middlesex."

SUNDAY 26th OCTOBER 1890

One of Middlesex's most noted pre-20th century batsmen, Henry William (Harry) Lee, was born in Marylebone, London. Lee's Middlesex career ran from 1911 until 1934, although it was interrupted by the First World War. He played for Middlesex in 401 first-class matches, scoring 18,594 runs at an average of 29.94. While not always noted for his flair, Lee was most certainly a prolific run scorer, reaching a century in 35 of his Middlesex innings and a double century on three separate occasions. Lee's run tally for Middlesex is all the more remarkable given that he nearly lost his life during the Great War, as a result of being shot in the thigh by the enemy, fracturing his femur, and being given up as for dead for three days before being captured by the Germans between the lines at Fleurbaix. He was transported through France and onto Hanover, where he was held until his release in 1915. He was discharged from the army with a Silver War badge to his name, and resumed his cricket career with Middlesex once again.

THURSDAY 26th OCTOBER 2006

Middlesex announced that Richard Johnson was to leave Somerset and return to the club for the 2007 season, after he had initially left Middlesex and joined the West Country side at the end of the 2000 season. Johnson had played six seasons with Somerset and was fondly remembered by Middlesex fans as the last bowler to take ten opposition wickets in an innings for the club in 1994.

SUNDAY 26th OCTOBER 2008

Having won the Twenty20 Cup at the Rose Bowl in June, Middlesex's reward was entry into the Stanford Super Series, played at the impressive Stanford Cricket Ground in Coolidge, Antigua. In their opening fixture against England, Middlesex lost the toss and were asked to field by England on a slow flat wicket. England struggled with the conditions and crawled to just 121 for four in their 20 overs. Ironically, Middlesex's Owais Shah top-scored for England with 39 not out. In reply, Middlesex struggled in equal measure and at no stage in their innings looked like getting ahead of the run rate. England ran out winners by 12 runs after Middlesex could only reach 109 for four in their innings.

FRIDAY 27th OCTOBER 2006

Having undergone and recovered from surgery at the end of the 2005 season following a severe back complaint, Middlesex announced the re-signing of Chad Keegan for the 2007 season. Keegan had undergone an extensive period of rehabilitation before rejoining the club, but never reclaimed the kind of form he had shown earlier in his career and made just six List-A appearances, failing to make a single first-class appearance.

MONDAY 27th OCTOBER 2008

Middlesex's second match in the Stanford Super Series was against Trinidad and Tobago, earning their place at the tournament as winners of the Caribbean domestic Twenty20 competition. This game had an extra edge to it, as Sir Allen Stanford had put up $400,000 in prize money for the winning team. Playing on exactly the same wicket as they had two days beforehand, Middlesex hadn't learnt any lessons, posting just 117 in their 20 overs, with only Eoin Morgan and Neil Dexter making any headway, scoring 30 and 39 respectively. Middlesex looked in control of things in the Trinidad innings, and had them at 49 for four after 11 overs until the West Indies keeper, Denesh Ramdin, came to the crease and launched a quickfire 41 off 28 balls to win the game and the cash for Trinidad in the final over.

WEDNESDAY 28th OCTOBER 1925

Charles King Francis, who represented Middlesex between 1875 and 1877, passed away on this day in Crichel, Dorset. Francis' Middlesex record was unremarkable in itself, but his achievements playing for Rugby School against Marlborough College in a match at Lord's make him stand out. He delivered what is probably the greatest ever individual performance in a public schools match in the history of the game. In the Marlborough College first innings, Francis returned figures of seven for 25 from 22 overs, six of them clean bowled, and in their second innings he took all ten wickets, nine of them clean bowled, to claim figures of ten for 15 from 23.2 overs. In all he'd taken 17 for 40 from 45.3 overs in the match. For Middlesex he was less prolific, taking 31 first-class wickets at 26.74 from the nine matches he played for the club.

WEDNESDAY 29th OCTOBER 2003

England's first ever tour to Bangladesh saw the second Test match in a two-match series start on this day, in the MA Aziz Stadium in Chittagong. Middlesex's Richard Johnson was in the tour party, although he missed out on selection in the opening Test match between the two countries, which England won by seven wickets. England won this second Test just as comfortably as the first, with Middlesex's Johnson claiming the man of the match award having taken five for 49 in Bangladesh's first innings and four for 44 in their second. His figures of nine for 92 were his best Test match figures for England and helped secure a 329-run victory.

THURSDAY 30th OCTOBER 2008

Middlesex's final match of the Stanford Super Series saw them up against Sir Allen Stanford's very own select XI, the Stanford Super Stars, who in all but name resembled a very strong West Indies international side. The Superstars were put into bat and looked to be struggling to post a big score at 126 for four in the 18th over, before Kieron Pollard and Andre Fletcher launched an astonishing assault on the Middlesex bowlers that took the Superstars score to a huge 173 from their 20 overs. In reply Middlesex never looked in it and stuttered along, before being bowled out for just 115 to lose by 58 runs. The Superstars went on to also thrash England with some ease in the $20 million showpiece match, winning by a convincing ten-wicket margin.

FRIDAY 31st OCTOBER 1986

Middlesex's captain, Mike Gatting, led his England side into an Ashes warm-up match against South Australia at the Adelaide Oval with Middlesex's John Emburey and Phil Edmonds in the side. Winning the toss, South Australia posted a total of 305, with Emburey taking three for 76. England made 407 in reply before South Australia again succumbed to Emburey, who took six for 102 as the hosts were bowled out for 269. England achieved their target of 168 for the loss of five wickets, with Emburey in at the end to score the winnings runs. Little did they know at this stage that Gatting would join a handful of England captains to lead an Ashes-winning side in Australia.

MIDDLESEX CCC
On This Day

NOVEMBER

MONDAY 1st NOVEMBER 1993

The Middlesex general committee and membership committee propose and agree in a meeting at Lord's that for the first time in the club's history they will introduce a 'joining fee' for all new members joining the club. The move fell in line with the policies already adopted by the majority of other first-class counties, but it was long debated at committee level. The one-off joining fee would be payable for all new membership applications received by the club after 1st January 1994 and would not be charged to existing members. Full membership of Middlesex CCC at this time stood at just £60 per annum.

FRIDAY 2nd NOVEMBER 1951

It wasn't until England's tour of India in 1951/1952 that a Middlesex player had the opportunity to play for their country in the sub-continent, as no Middlesex contingent had been present in England's successful tour of India in 1933, when they won the three-match series 2-0. Middlesex batsman Jack Robertson was included in the touring party in the 1951 tour and played in each of the five Tests in the series, which began in Delhi. Robertson kicked off the tour with a half century in the first Test and totalled 310 runs on the tour, at an average of 38.75. The series ended 1-1, with three draws and one win for each side.

WEDNESDAY 3rd NOVEMBER 1852

Arguably one of the briefest of all Middlesex careers was that of Edmund Harvey, who was born on this day in Islington, north London. Harvey made first-class appearances for four different teams, yet bizarrely played only once for each side, and all four games were played in just a three-week period. Harvey made his debut in first-class cricket for an England XI playing against Cambridge University at Fenner's in May 1927. He then played for a Gentlemen of England XI against the same opposition the following week. The very next week he played for Middlesex, just once, against the MCC, getting ducks in both Middlesex innings at Lord's before finishing his 'career' in mid June 1927 with a fixture against the MCC for Cambridge University this time – finishing again with a duck in the second innings. After four matches he never played again.

WEDNESDAY 4th NOVEMBER 2009

The club announced the signing of fast bowler Tobias Skelton (Toby) Roland-Jones to the Middlesex playing ranks for the 2010 season. Roland-Jones had performed well for the Middlesex second XI throughout the 2009 season and was rightly rewarded with a full playing contract as a result. The little known Roland-Jones, at just 22 years of age, made his first-class debut against the Oxford University Centre of Cricketing Excellence in May, taking 2-11 from ten overs before bursting onto the County Championship scene for Middlesex in June. He took an impressive 38 wickets in his first season in the Middlesex side, playing in eight County Championship matches with an average of just 19.60, finishing joint top of the wicket taking column alongside Tim Murtagh.

TUESDAY 5th NOVEMBER 1861

Sir Timothy Carew (Tim) O'Brien 3rd Baronet was born in Dublin, Ireland. Carew was a free scoring and forceful right-handed batsman who played for Middlesex between the years of 1881 and 1898, making 156 first-class appearances for the club. He scored an impressive 7,377 runs at an average of 29.63, which was enough to earn him a call-up to the England Test side for the tour to South Africa under Lord Hawke in 1896. He was surprised to be elected as captain in the first Test match of the series against South Africa and, while not having an outstanding match himself, he successfully captained the side to victory, although it was thanks largely to the efforts of George Lohmann, who took 15 wickets for 45 runs for England. O'Brien had an individual top score of 202 runs for Middlesex, which he scored against Sussex in 1895 at Hove's County Ground.

SATURDAY 6th NOVEMBER 1999

Generally thought of as the best wicketkeeper-batsman the game has ever seen, Adam Gilchrist, who played for Middlesex in their 2010 Twenty20 campaign, made his Test debut for Australia on this day in the opening Test match of a three-match series against Pakistan. At the Gabba in Brisbane, Gilchrist hit a rapid 81 runs from just 88 balls before being bowled by Shoaib Akhtar. He then took six catches behind the stumps as Australia won the match by a convincing ten wickets.

TUESDAY 7th NOVEMBER 1876

An extraordinary general meeting focused primarily on the difficulties Middlesex were experiencing with their current home ground, following ongoing disputes with their current landowner. The MCC's secretary Henry Perkins had put forward a proposal for Middlesex to share their Lord's ground in St John's Wood, which now seemingly appeared to be the only sensible option to consider. Chief opposition to the idea came from Isaac (ID) Walker, who had serious doubts over the financial implications of such a move. So strong was the feeling of the Middlesex players, however, that Walker withdrew his opposition. The proposal was unanimously voted for after it was presented, and Middlesex County Cricket Club had a new permanent home at Lord's.

SUNDAY 8th NOVEMBER 1987

An England side captained by Middlesex's Mike Gatting, including his county teammates Paul Downton and John Emburey, reached the final of the Reliance Cricket World Cup, played at Eden Gardens in Calcutta. Gatting's men had reached the final after beating co-hosts India in the semi-final and finishing second in their group behind Pakistan. In the final, arch enemies Australia were the opposition, who themselves had beaten Pakistan in the other semi-final. Batting first, Australia, under Allan Border, posted a total of 253 in their 50 overs, and then restricted England to just 246 in reply, with Gatting hitting a quickfire 41 runs. Australia edged the most closely-fought World Cup final to date, winning by just seven runs to lift the trophy. Gatting's side were the second England team to reach a World Cup final and lose.

THURSDAY 9th NOVEMBER 2006

Following Ben Hutton's resignation from the captaincy a month earlier, the club announced that Ed Smith was to be immediately appointed to the role of captain. Smith, already an established member of the Middlesex side, relished the opportunity to take the side forward and stated that he looked forward to a successful period at the helm of the club. While relatively short, his record was impressive as captain, losing only four of the 23 matches he captained Middlesex in. Smith retired from the game and the club captaincy in 2008 after a serious injury which forced him to miss most of the season.

MONDAY 10th NOVEMBER 1856

John Thomas Rawlin, who played for Middlesex between 1889 and 1909, was born on this day in Rotherham, Yorkshire. Rawlin was a solid right-handed batsman and a useful right-arm fast-medium bowler. After starting his first-class career with Yorkshire, Rawlin moved south and joined the MCC ground staff in 1887, enabling him to qualify for Middlesex on residential grounds. He represented Middlesex for more than two decades, making 229 first-class appearances and scoring 5,680 runs at an average of 17.37, as well as taking 649 wickets at an average of only 20.45. He took ten wickets in a match on ten occasions for the club, and took five wickets in an innings on 35 occasions.

WEDNESDAY 11th NOVEMBER 1998

The Middlesex CCC committee agreed upon the launch of an ambitious new youth cricket development programme, entitled 'Crusade for Cricket', which saw the club invest heavily in the development of youth cricket within Middlesex with a view to significantly increasing the participation levels of youngsters aged between eight and 18 in the county. The launch of the scheme, planned for early 1999, coincided with the arrival of 'one-day' names for first-class counties, so to work in tandem with the youth scheme and to assist with its awareness, it was agreed that Middlesex CCC's one-day side would be known from here on as the 'Crusaders'. This remained the case until the club rebranded its one-day side to become the Panthers in 2009.

MONDAY 12th NOVEMBER 2007

Following the untimely departure of first XI head coach Richard Pybus midway through the season, the vacant role had been temporarily filled jointly by Middlesex's former academy director and second XI coach, Toby Radford, and Middlesex's director of cricket, John Emburey. In the close season of 2007, Radford was appointed permanently as Middlesex's new head coach, following a successful period with the first XI in the latter stages of the season. Like Pybus before him, Radford's tenure was relatively short, but he did successfully coach the side to their first major trophy for 15 years, when he led Middlesex to Twenty20 Cup success in 2008 before resigning from the post in the middle of the 2009 season, citing a change in his responsibilities after the appointment of captain Shaun Udal.

FRIDAY 13th NOVEMBER 2009

In a Twenty20 International against South Africa, Middlesex's Eoin Morgan scored the highest ever individual Twenty20 innings by an England batsman, when he smashed the ball to all parts of the New Wanderers Stadium in Johannesburg on his way to a brilliant 85 not out against a very good South African attack. In Morgan's innings he faced just 45 balls and blasted seven fours and five sixes to help England to a total of 202 in their 20 overs. In an extremely tight game, England secured victory by the narrow margin of just one run after South Africa could only manage to score 127 in their rain affected innings of 13 overs, which had been adjusted by the Duckworth Lewis method. Morgan has to date collected 16 International Twenty20 caps, and has a staggering average of 47.30, having scored 473 runs, with a strike rate of 134.75.

FRIDAY 14th NOVEMBER 1930

Alan Edward Moss, Middlesex's eighth-highest first-class wicket taker of all time, was born in Tottenham, London. Moss's Middlesex career spanned the years 1950 to 1963, during which he took an incredible 1,088 first-class wickets at an average of 19.81. Moss's best first-class bowling performance for Middlesex came when he took 8-31 against Northamptonshire at Kettering in July 1960. Amazingly, just a month earlier he had also taken eight wickets in an innings, claiming 8-37 against Glamorgan at The Gnoll, Neath. Moss's consistency for Middlesex was rewarded with a Test call-up by England, who he went on to play nine Test matches for, taking 21 wickets at an average of 29.80. Moss serves to this day on the Middlesex executive board, and he has held the positions of president, treasurer and chairman on the Middlesex committee since he retired from playing in 1968.

FRIDAY 15th NOVEMBER 1996

The club announced the news that a lucrative long-term principal sponsorship agreement had been negotiated and agreed with asset management company, Hill Samuel. The new deal replaced the existing Panasonic sponsorship, which had been secured as a short-term solution for the previous season, and would see the Hill Samuel Asset Management logo appearing on all Middlesex playing kit for at least the next three years.

EOIN JOSEPH GERARD MORGAN – ONE OF ENGLAND'S BRIGHTEST ONE-DAY TALENTS OF THE MODERN ERA

TUESDAY 16th NOVEMBER 1982

Middlesex pace bowler Norman Cowans made his debut for England in the opening Test of the Ashes series in Australia in 1982, as England under Bob Willis looked to win their fourth successive Ashes series. Cowans, brought into the side purely for his bowling firepower, was definitely not known for his batting abilities, as his first-class batting average for Middlesex stood at just 9.26. Despite this, he managed to put on a partnership of 66 runs for the final wicket of England's second innings with Derek Pringle, scoring 36 runs himself, to take England from 292 for nine to a respectable 358 all out, much to the annoyance of two of the world's greatest bowlers, Dennis Lillee and Terry Alderman. England earned a draw in the match thanks to Cowans' heroics.

TUESDAY 17th NOVEMBER 1863

The birth of Middlesex County Cricket Club can be traced back to an autumn afternoon on this day, when a group of gentlemen met to inspect the suitability of a ground in Copenhagen Fields, Islington, north London, owned by inn-keeper Thomas Norris, hoping that this could become the permanent home ground of a newly-formed Middlesex County Cricket Club. The group included two of the Walker brothers, John and Vyell, C. Gordon, W. Nicholson and C. Hillyard, among others. Professional cricketers Fred and James Lillywhite were also in attendance to offer advice on the ground conditions where necessary. On agreeing that the ground was deemed to be a suitable venue, the party agreed to meet the following week.

WEDNESDAY 18th NOVEMBER 2009

Middlesex announced the arrival of a genuine legend of the game, Adam Gilchrist, who was signed to play for the Panthers in five of their 2010 Twenty20 matches at Lord's. Gilchrist eventually played eight matches in Middlesex's 2010 season, seven in the club's Twenty20 campaign and once against the touring Australians at Lord's. While with Middlesex, Gilchrist scored 212 runs in 20 matches at an average of 30.28, and 38 runs against the Australians in the tour match. Gilchrist took over the captaincy of the club from Shaun Udal after just two matches, leading out the side at Canterbury, where he scored a 47-ball century for the Panthers to win the match.

WEDNESDAY 19th NOVEMBER 1879

Harry Robert (Joe) Murrell was born in Hounslow, Middlesex. Murrell was a competent batsman and exceptional wicketkeeper who represented Middlesex between the years of 1906 and 1926. He scored more than 6,000 runs for the club at an average of just under 15, with a highest score of 96 not out. It was behind the stumps where Murrell was most effective, taking a total of 516 catches and 263 stumpings for the club in his Middlesex career. Following his retirement from a prestigious playing career, Murrell rejoined the club in 1946, and became the first XI official scorer until his death in August 1952, whereupon the role was taken over by Middlesex legend Patsy Hendren until 1960.

SATURDAY 20th NOVEMBER 1971

New Zealand Test and One-Day International all-rounder Dion Joseph Nash was born in Auckland, New Zealand. Nash joined Middlesex in the 1995 season and made a solid start to his Middlesex career, taking 52 first-class wickets in his first full season with the club, also scoring 433 runs at an average of nearly 21, including three half centuries. Unfortunately, early in his second year with the club, Nash suffered a serious injury which ruled him out for all but one of Middlesex's Championship matches in the season, and the club had no alternative but to release him at the end of his contract.

SATURDAY 21st NOVEMBER 1970

One of Australian cricket's finest opening batsmen, Justin Lee Langer, was born in Perth, Western Australia. Langer scored more than 7,500 Test runs for Australia at an average of 45.27 in a career spanning 1992 to 2007. Langer joined Middlesex in the season of 1998 and played until the end of the 2000 season, captaining the side in his final year. Langer's maiden hundred in English cricket was a magnificent innings of 233 not out against Somerset at Lord's in only his third first-class appearance for the club. He scored more than 1,000 first-class runs in each of the three seasons he spent with Middlesex, with his best season coming in 1998, scoring 1,448 first-class runs. In 43 first-class appearances for the club he made 3,968 runs at an average of 61.04, including 13 centuries.

FRIDAY 22nd NOVEMBER 1991

Middlesex County Cricket Club announced that they had reached agreement on a new principal sponsorship agreement for the club with global consumer healthcare company Smithkline Beecham. The deal was for an initial three-year term of principal sponsorship of Middlesex, and would see Middlesex players' sweaters bearing the Smithkline Beecham brand name in all forms of the game. The new sponsorship agreement also meant that the Middlesex president at the time, Denis Compton, would once again resume his association with the brand which saw him labelled as 'The Brylcrem Boy' at the height of his playing career.

WEDNESDAY 23rd NOVEMBER 1994

Long serving Middlesex bowler Neil 'Nelly' Williams announced that he was leaving Middlesex to join up with Essex CCC, having signed a new three-year deal with the county. Williams took 479 first-class wickets for Middlesex in his time at the club and was considered to be a difficult character to replace, not only for his excellence on the field, but also for his popularity off the field. Having won the County Championship title as recently as 1993, the Middlesex side for the 2005 season was beginning to look like a very different unit, facing life without their long-serving opening batsman, Desmond Haynes, and without one of their most consistent and prolific pace bowlers of the past decade in Neil Williams.

THURSDAY 24th NOVEMBER 1932

Legendary Middlesex and England bowler – although many would say he more than deserved all-rounder status – Frederick John (Fred) Titmus was born in Kentish Town, London. Titmus's career at Middlesex was truly the stuff of legend. His 2,361 wickets, at an average of just 21.27, included five wickets in an innings on 146 separate occasions, positioning him as the club's all time leading wicket taker. He was no less prolific with the bat, scoring 17,320 first-class runs for the club, which puts him 13th in the all-time leading run scorers list at a healthy average of 22.78. Titmus's first-class Middlesex career took off in 1949 and didn't end until 33 years later, across five different decades, when he signed off with figures of three for 43 in his final match for Middlesex, a victory against Surrey in 1982.

THURSDAY 25th NOVEMBER 2010

The opening match of the 2010 Ashes series kicked off in Brisbane, Australia, with Middlesex's Andrew Strauss leading an England squad including fellow Middlesex men Steven Finn and Eoin Morgan. Morgan missed out on selection for the first Test, but Strauss captained a side including Finn to a well-earned draw as England kicked off their defence of the Ashes. Things started badly for Strauss, falling for a third-ball duck as England were dismissed for just 260 on the opening day. Middlesex's Finn then took career best Test bowling figures of six for 125 in the Australian first innings as the home side were dismissed for 481 to take a lead of 221 into the second innings. Strauss redeemed himself with a fine knock of 110 in England's second innings, as England scored a record-breaking 517 for one to kill off the game and earn a hard-fought draw.

THURSDAY 26th NOVEMBER 1863

The 'formation party' of John and Vyell Walker, Gordon, Nicholson, Hillyard, and landowner Norris met again at the Cattle Market Ground in Islington and agreed that Mr C. Hillyard would stand as provisional honorary secretary. It was decreed that he would send a notice to the Sporting press, including *Bell's Life*, *Sporting Life* and the *Sporting Gazette*, to inform all existing clubs and all the 'gentlemen' of Middlesex of their intention to establish a county club. The notice expressed the sentiment that as "a feeling has long existed that a Middlesex County Club should be established", a meeting would be held on Tuesday 15th December at the London Tavern in Bishopsgate.

THURSDAY 27th NOVEMBER 2008

At the 11th hour, Middlesex's scheduled Champions League T20 trip was thrown into complete turmoil, as overnight terrorist atrocities in Mumbai, India, forced the club to delay their flights to India and seek advice from the Foreign Office. In Mumbai, terrorists launched a gunfire attack, killing and wounding tourists within the Taj Mahal Hotel, the very same hotel that the Middlesex team were planning on staying at just 24 hours later. The club released a statement advising fans and members that their travel plans were on hold, awaiting further news, and that the players' safety would come first in any decision the club made on travelling to India.

MONDAY 28th NOVEMBER 1966

In Middlesex's history, less than 30 batsmen have scored more than 10,000 runs for the club. One of them, Michael Anthony (Mike) Roseberry, was born in Houghton-le-Spring, County Durham. Roseberry, who played for Middlesex between 1985 and 2001, formed a hugely successful opening partnership with West Indian Desmond Haynes from 1989 until 1994. He was an essential part of the County Championship-winning sides of 1990 and 1993 and of the one-day trophy winning teams of the generation, scoring a total of 10,010 runs for the club at 36.00. His most successful season for Middlesex came in 1992, his benefit year, when he scored 2,044 first-class runs at an average of 56.77.

WEDNESDAY 29th NOVEMBER 1989

The club and all within the game mourned the loss of 'Mr Cricket', Sir George Oswald Browning (Gubby) Allen, who died, aged 87, in his St John's Wood home overlooking his beloved Lord's. Upon finishing his playing career in 1950, Allen became one of the most influential administrators in the game, fulfilling roles as chairman of the TCCB England selection panel – or the ECB as they are known today – president and treasurer of Marylebone Cricket Club, and serving a long term on the Middlesex committee, including a two-year term as club president between 1977 and 1979. Allen was knighted with a CBE for 'services to the game' in 1986 and a stand alongside the Lord's pavilion, which houses the Middlesex Room, is named in his honour.

TUESDAY 30th NOVEMBER 1954

Both Denis Compton and Bill Edrich were part of the England side which travelled with an Ashes party to Australia, looking to be the first England side to win in Australia for 21 years. Things started badly as Australia thrashed them in Brisbane in the opening Test, with both Compton and Edrich playing for England. Edrich performed admirably, scoring 88 in the England second innings, but Compton, suffering an injury, batted at number 11 in England's first innings, scoring two not out, then at number ten in England's second innings, when he fell for a duck. Despite losing the opening Test England's fortunes turned around, and after this disastrous start they went on to win the series 3-1, with Compton playing injured through much of the tour.

MIDDLESEX CCC
On This Day

DECEMBER

FRIDAY 1st DECEMBER 1871

The Middlesex committee met at the University Club, Jermyn Street, London to discuss the suitability of the club's then home ground in Lillie Bridge. It was unanimously agreed that the isolated location and poor pitch conditions dictated a move to a new ground. The choice of new ground was the Prince's Ground, near Hans Place, London. Middlesex player at the time, Edward Rutter, wrote this of the club's new home: "It was a large open space in the midst of a fast growing district, at the back of Harrods and very accessible. The owners have developed it skilfully, and laid down excellent wickets. On one side of the ground a club had established itself, where society forgathered and practised roller skating, which was in vogue just then. It was very select, and no outsiders were admitted to that part; a great rendezvous for tea, and altogether a fashionable lounge. The cricket, however, was carefully looked after, the ground kept well, and the public had every convenience." The club were to spend the next five seasons at the Prince's Ground.

SATURDAY 2nd DECEMBER 1978

Having captained England to a 3-0 Ashes series win in England in 1977, Middlesex captain Mike Brearley led England to Australia to retain the Ashes. The opening Ashes Test in Brisbane saw Brearley lose the toss and field, but the decision was soon to backfire on the Australians as they were dismissed for just 116. England's reply netted them 286 runs to lead by 170 runs. Australia rallied and posted 339 in their second innings, but England reached their winning target for the loss of three wickets to win the opening Test. England went 1-0 up and Brearley's 100% record as captain in Ashes Tests continued.

FRIDAY 2nd DECEMBER 2010

The ECB announced that Middlesex's Umesh Valjee would captain the England deaf cricket team on the winter Ashes tour to Australia. Valjee would lead the side in one Ashes Test, two One-Day Internationals and three International Twenty20 matches, in a triangular tournament with Australia and South Africa in Geelong. England would be looking to reclaim the Deaf Ashes, which Australia were in possession of. This would be the first time that Middlesex had two players in Australia captaining an England Ashes tour side at the same time.

SUNDAY 3rd DECEMBER 1995

After nearly 25 years of loyal service as a player for Middlesex, John Emburey accepted a deal to join Northamptonshire for the 1996 and 1997 seasons, with a view to taking on a more managerial focused role. The Middlesex committee were keen to retain Emburey's services as a player, and as such had registered him as a List I category player, offering him a lucrative new two-year playing contract. At Emburey's own request, the contract offer from Middlesex was withdrawn, and the Middlesex committee allowed Emburey, one of its greatest servants, to leave the club to fulfil his desire to move into coaching and management with Northamptonshire.

TUESDAY 4th DECEMBER 2007

Middlesex signed the experienced off spinner and England international, Shaun Udal, from Hampshire. After serving Hampshire for 18 years and making four Test and 11 One-Day International appearances for England, Udal had reached his decision to retire from the first-class game at the age of 38, and was destined to play for minor counties side Berkshire. In need of an experienced off spinner, Middlesex's director of cricket, John Emburey, contacted Udal and coaxed him out of retirement to join Middlesex. Udal proved a popular addition to the Middlesex dressing room, and took on the club captaincy from Ed Smith in 2008.

SATURDAY 5th DECEMBER 2009

Middlesex's new overseas signing for the 2010 season was New Zealand Test-capped pace bowler Iain O'Brien. O'Brien initially joined the club on a three-year deal, with a view to completing his first year as an overseas signing, then qualifying locally as a domestic cricketer, given that he was residing in the UK and was married to an English woman. Unfortunately the ECB denied O'Brien the opportunity to register as a local cricketer after failing to meet their criteria for domestic registration. An appeal process to the ECB, backed by the club, also failed to satisfy them, and O'Brien was left out in the cold after one year with the club.

WEDNESDAY 6th DECEMBER 2006

Middlesex announced the signing of medium-fast bowler Tim Murtagh from Surrey. Murtagh, then aged 25, was seen as a relatively uninspired signing, having taken just 68 first-class wickets at an average of 37.72 in the 34 matches he'd played in six years at Surrey. The move to Middlesex transformed Murtagh's career, as he led the Middlesex attack and bowled his way to the club's Player of the Year award for the next three consecutive seasons. In 2007 he took 42 wickets at 24.85, in 2008 64 wickets at 27.09, and in 2009 60 wickets at 25.35. Since joining Middlesex he has taken a total of 204 first-class wickets at just 27.96.

THURSDAY 7th DECEMBER 1995

In both 1990 and 1991 the issue of whether Middlesex lady members should be allowed access to the Lord's pavilion on match days had been discussed by the Middlesex committee. On both occasions, the MCC had reached a decision against making a change to their existing rules, which excluded ladies from entering the pavilion. In 1995 the committee felt strongly that the issue should again be raised, and Middlesex members were canvassed to gain feedback on the proposition. The results that came back surprised everyone, as out of over 1,050 replies received from male members, only 51% were in favour of the proposition. Even more surprisingly, 31% of lady members were against it. The committee decided to shelve their plans due to an apparent lack of support from the club's members.

TUESDAY 8th DECEMBER 1936

One of only nine players in history to have surpassed the 20,000 first-class runs mark for Middlesex, Peter Howard Parfitt, was born in Billingham, Norfolk. In a Middlesex playing career between 1956 and 1972, Parfitt scored 21,302 first-class runs at 36.66. Parfitt captained the side between 1968 and 1970 and to this day is still actively involved with Middlesex CCC, sitting on the club's executive board as president. Parfitt made 37 Test appearances for England, scoring an impressive 1,882 runs at an average of 40.91. Parfitt was widely regarded as one of the finest stroke-players of his day, and also took 231 wickets for Middlesex at an average of 27.80.

WEDNESDAY 9th DECEMBER 1987

Middlesex captain Mike Gatting was at the centre of an international cricket row as Test umpire Shakoor Rana refused to take to the field when playing against Gatting's England side in Faisalabad, Pakistan. No play took place on the third day of the Test, as both Rana and Gatting were demanding apologies from each other following two furious arguments and accusations that cheating had taken place on the field of play the previous day. After tense behind-the-scenes discussions Rana would still not take to the field, so play was suspended for the entire day. Play eventually resumed on day four but, with so much time taken out of the match, a draw was the inevitable result.

SUNDAY 10th DECEMBER 1933

Robert Alex (Bob) Gale was born in Old Warden, Bedfordshire. Gale was a swashbuckling batsman who played in 219 first-class matches for Middlesex, scoring 11,234 runs at an average of 29.10 between 1956 and 1965, including 13 centuries and a highest score of 200 made against Glamorgan in 1962. After retiring from Middlesex in 1965, Gale continued his association with the club, serving on the Middlesex committee as chairman for nine years and president for three. Gale's run tally puts him in the top 25 run scorers of all time for the club.

SATURDAY 11th DECEMBER 1880

Francis Albert (Frank) Tarrant, one of Middlesex's greatest all-rounders, was born in Melbourne, Australia. Tarrant's first-class record for Middlesex between 1904 and 1914 saw him score 12,169 runs at an average of 38.02 and take 1,005 wickets at an average of 17.43. Tarrant's final year with the club, 1914, was his most memorable, as he scored back-to-back double hundreds against Essex and Worcestershire, with 250* and 200 respectively. He followed this up with one of the greatest all round performances the game has ever seen, taking 16 for 176 and scoring 101 not out in a match against Lancashire. Staggeringly though, this wasn't Tarrant's finest all round performance of his career, which he saved for the unfortunate opponents of Lord Willingdon's XI. When playing in India in 1918 for the Maharajah of Cooch-Behar's XI, he took all ten of the Willingdon first-innings wickets, and then proceeded to smash their bowlers for an unbeaten 182.

MONDAY 12th DECEMBER 1887

Born in Kensington, London, Nigel Esme Haig regularly represented Middlesex for more than two decades in a career spanning 1912 to 1934, seeing him captain the side for six seasons. Haig was one of the most reliable and consistent all-rounders of his generation, racking up 12,289 runs and taking 931 wickets in a long Middlesex career in which he represented the county on 417 occasions. Haig achieved the all-rounders double on three separate occasions, scoring 1,000 runs and taking 100 wickets in the 1921, 1927 and 1929 seasons.

SATURDAY 13th DECEMBER 2008

Following the Mumbai terrorist atrocities towards the end of the previous month, the Board of Cricket Control for India (BCCI) eventually announced that the inaugural Champions League T20 competition was cancelled amid severe threats of further terrorist acts in India and an inability to guarantee the safety of those teams taking part, which was nothing short of a huge blow for Middlesex both financially and logistically. Middlesex's chief executive stated on hearing the news: "We are naturally very disappointed that the event has been cancelled as we were excited about being the English representatives in this unique, inaugural tournament. We will just have to go out and win the domestic Twenty20 again so that we can compete in the Champions League next year." Alas this wasn't to be however, as the club failed to qualify for finals day the next year.

TUESDAY 14th DECEMBER 1897

Middlesex's John Thomas (Jack) Hearne shone for England in Australia in the opening Test match of the 1897/1898 Ashes series, played at the Sydney Cricket Ground on this day. England put on a massive 551 in their first innings before Australia started batting on the second day. By the end of day two, Hearne had picked up three Australian wickets, finishing with five for 42 as the hosts were dismissed for just 237. Following on, Australia fared slightly better, scoring 409 in their second innings with Hearne taking another four for 99. England knocked off the runs for the loss of just one wicket to take a lead in the series. Sadly they lost the remaining four Tests and the series 4-1. Hearne played in all five Ashes Tests and took an impressive 20 wickets.

TUESDAY 15th DECEMBER 1863

Following the notice placed in the sporting press in November, a meeting was held in the London Tavern, Bishopsgate, chaired by The Hon Robert Grimston, in which the informal founding of Middlesex County Cricket Club was discussed. It was agreed that "no county club be formed for Middlesex until at least 100 persons have promised to join it", and "that a further meeting be called as soon as the requisite number of names have been forwarded to Mr Hillyard." As a result of the notice posted in the sporting press, Hillyard had already received more than 100 names for consideration for membership of a new club, so a provisional committee was appointed and a notice was placed in the leading newspapers of the day to notify those within the county that a general meeting would take place the following year, on 2nd February, to officially constitute the club. Hillyard also wrote to the ground owner, Norris, informing him of the intention to establish the club and make use of his land as the club's home ground.

FRIDAY 16th DECEMBER 1903

Middlesex's Pelham Warner was tasked with regaining the Ashes for England from the dominant Australians, who had won the previous four Ashes series. Warner had Middlesex's Bernard Bosanquet in his side, who had famously invented the googly delivery which was proving so effective on home soil. The first Test in Sydney went England's way, with Bosanquet picking up three of the Australian wickets, as England won the opening Test by five wickets. Warner's side successfully went on to reclaim the Ashes, taking claim of the urn for the first time since 1896, winning the series 3-2, with Warner himself scoring 239 runs in the series and Bosanquet picking up 16 wickets.

FRIDAY 17th DECEMBER 1976

Consistent form for Middlesex earned batsman Graham Barlow a Test call-up to the England side for the tour to India, led by Middlesex's Mike Brearley. Barlow had hit nearly 1,500 runs the previous season at an average of nearly 50, so went into the tour in particularly good form. Sadly his run scoring didn't continue and, after innings of 0, 4, 7*, 1 and 5 in his first three Test matches, Barlow never appeared for England again.

MONDAY 18th DECEMBER 1933

Middlesex all-rounder Donald (Don) Bennett was born in Wakefield, Yorkshire. Making his debut at 16 in 1950, Bennett played for Middlesex for 18 years. In his Middlesex first-class career he scored more than 10,000 runs at 21.85, and took 748 wickets at 26.45. Bennett's impressive playing career was surpassed by his services to the club as a coach, a role in which he excelled for 29 years, guiding the club through the most successful period in its history before stepping down in 1997. Bennett has maintained links with the club since then, serving on the Middlesex committee in a number of leading roles to this very day.

MONDAY 19th DECEMBER 1994

Middlesex opening batsman Mike Roseberry announced his decision to leave the club after eight years. Roseberry had his eyes turned when receiving a close-season offer from his home county of Durham to join them as their captain. Roseberry's contribution to Middlesex CCC was impressive and, after an unsuccessful period in the North East with Durham, he was welcomed back to play for Middlesex again between 1999 and 2001.

THURSDAY 20th DECEMBER 1894

The first Middlesex player to captain the England Test team, Andrew Stoddart, led his side on a brilliant 3-2 Ashes series win, with the opening timeless Test finishing on this day in Sydney. Australia posted a first-innings total of 586 before dismissing England for 325 in reply. With England 261 behind, Australia's captain, John Blackham, enforced the follow-on, and England were dismissed for 437. This left the Australians needing just 177 for a series opening win, and they had comfortably reached 113 for two at the close of day five. Blackham agreed to start day six 20 minutes late, as two England players, including Robert Peel, were late to the ground suffering from hangovers. This would be a decision that Blackham would regret as, amazingly, Peel went on to take six for 67, and Stoddart's men dismissed Australia for just 166 to secure a win by just ten runs, becoming the first side ever to win a Test match having been made to follow on. Middlesex's Francis Gilbertson Ford also made his England Test debut in this match, scoring 30 and 48 in England's two innings.

TUESDAY 21st DECEMBER 1993

The club announced the resignation of Michael Sturt, who had unexpectedly and suddenly stepped down as the club's chairman. Sturt had only been in office for a matter of months, having been voted in at the club's AGM in April, but he had been a long-standing member of the Middlesex committee. Sturt's tenure of only eight months in the chair ended with him citing "a matter of principle" as the reason behind his resignation, and he left the club and ended his long association with Middlesex with immediate effect.

SUNDAY 22nd DECEMBER 1996

England's first ever Test match against Zimbabwe ended in thrilling circumstances on this day. The match, played at Queens Sports Club, Bulawayo, saw an England side which included Middlesex's Phil Tufnell going into the Test expecting to win. Tufnell himself went into the match in great form, having taken 78 first-class wickets for Middlesex in the 1996 domestic season, which he continued when taking two for 76 in Zimbabwe's first innings of 376. England then scored 406 before Tufnell again got in on the action, taking four for 61 as Zimbabwe made 234 in their second innings. England needed 205 to win the match, although time was against them. With only 37 overs of play left on the final day, it came down to England needing three runs off the final ball of the match to win. They managed just two and the scores were tied and for the first time ever a Test match was drawn with the scores level.

FRIDAY 23rd DECEMBER 1977

Middlesex captain Mike Brearley led England into their first ever One-Day International fixture in Pakistan in Sahiwal in front of 15,000 screaming Pakistani spectators. His side included his Middlesex teammates Mike Gatting, Paul Downton and Phil Edmonds. The match proved to be a closely fought encounter, with England winning off the final ball of the match. Brearley's men restricted the Pakistani side to 208, before knocking off the runs for the loss of seven wickets. England needed ten runs from the final over to win the match, and when Edmonds was run out for five with four balls remaining, it was left to Ian Botham to hit the winning runs and secure a magnificent and tense victory.

THURSDAY 24th DECEMBER 1867

Born on Christmas Eve in Skipton, Yorkshire, George Thornton played first-class cricket for Middlesex between the years of 1893 and 1899. Thornton was a left-handed all rounder who had his finest season with Middlesex in 1895, scoring 317 runs at an average of 31.70 and taking 23 wickets at an average of 28.56. His finest hour came when playing against Gloucestershire at Lord's that year, when he dismissed the great WG Grace, clean bowling him for 169. He took nine wickets in the game – four for 52 in the Gloucestershire first innings and five for 20 in the second.

TUESDAY 25th DECEMBER 1934

Middlesex middle-order batsman Gustave Peter Sapenne (Peter) Delisle was born on Christmas Day in Basseterre, St Kitts. Delisle played for Oxford University in the 1954, 1955 and 1956 seasons, but also joined Middlesex to play when he was on leave in university holidays. He played for the club in a total of 55 first-class matches, scoring 1,935 runs at an average of 21.50. His highest individual Middlesex score was 130, which he got against Cambridge University at Fenner's in 1957, and his finest season came in 1955, when he scored a total of 1,185 first-class runs in the season.

FRIDAY 26th DECEMBER 1986

Middlesex captain Mike Gatting led his England side into the fourth Ashes Test on Boxing Day 1-0 up in the series, knowing that an England victory in Melbourne would make him the first England captain to win an Ashes series in Australia since Middlesex's Mike Brearley achieved the feat back in 1978/79. Gatting had with him Middlesex's spin twins John Emburey and Phil Edmonds, who on a turning Melbourne track would eventually prove to be a key factor in the match. Gatting won the toss and put the Australians in to bat. Less than 55 overs later they were all out for just 141. In reply England made light work of overturning the deficit, recording a total of 349, with Gatting himself making a useful 40. Edmonds and Emburey then took five wickets between them as the Australians were dismissed for just 194. England went 2-0 up in the series with just one Test to play, in Sydney, and won the Ashes.

THURSDAY 27th DECEMBER 1984

Leslie Harry Compton, brother of Middlesex's Denis and great uncle of Nick, died on this day in Hendon, Middlesex at the age of 72. Like his brother, Leslie himself had a brilliant career as a professional with both Arsenal and Middlesex, although while Denis was undoubtedly the better cricketer of the two, Leslie was the more competent footballer. In Leslie's Middlesex playing career he appeared in the famous 1947 County Championship-winning side with Denis for Middlesex. Leslie scored a total of 5,781 runs and, as wicketkeeper, took an impressive 467 catches and 129 stumpings.

WEDNESDAY 28th DECEMBER 1870

A meeting of the club's committee at the Inns of Court Hotel, London concluded with the shock realisation that "a general meeting be called for the purpose of considering the advisability of continuing the club" due to lack of support from those within the county. At the time the finances were seriously in arrears and the club had already sold its pavilion to Richmond for £153 to raise funds and reduce the £204 deficit on the books. A special general meeting was therefore called, with all members notified that a vote would take place on January 18th 1871 to vote on whether the club could continue.

SATURDAY 29th DECEMBER 1894

As the first ever Middlesex player to captain the England Test side, Andrew Stoddart led from the front in the second Test of the 1894/95 Ashes series, when he scored a brilliant innings of 173 to win the match for England and put his side 2-0 up in the series. After losing the opening Test, having made England follow on, Australian captain John Blackham was replaced by George Giffen, but the new captain's fortunes did not improve. Winning the toss, Giffen became the first captain in Test history to put the opposition in to bat. It looked to have been a good decision as England were dismissed for just 75 in their first innings, but they immediately bounced back and knocked the Australians over for 123. It was in England's second innings that Stoddart came to the fore, as his 173 helped England reach 475. Needing 428 to win, Australia were dismissed for 333 and England won the Test by 94 runs.

SATURDAY 30th DECEMBER 1882

Brothers Charles Thomas Studd and George Brown Studd became the first ever Middlesex siblings to play in the same Test side for England, when they toured Australia and took part in the tour that became known as 'The quest to regain The Ashes', the first series between the two sides after the Test at the Oval when the Ashes had been 'created'. This was also the first time that four Middlesex players represented England in a Test side, as both George Frederick Vernon and Charles Frederick Leslie also appeared. All four played for IFW Bligh's England XI in the opening Test at Melbourne, where the Australians won by nine wickets. CT Studd took two for 35 as Australia were dismissed for 291 in their first innings, then scored 0 and 21 in England's two innings. His brother scored seven and 0. Vernon scored 11 not out and three, and Leslie took three for 31 with the ball, then scored four in both innings.

TUESDAY 31st DECEMBER 1985

There are probably more relaxing ways to spend a New Year's Eve, but Middlesex's Mike Gatting, Paul Downton, Phil Edmonds and Norman Cowans were all in the England team playing in the third Test of five against India at Eden Gardens, Calcutta in what, thanks largely to India captain Mohammed Azharuddin's negative tactics, turned into a near riot in the crowd. Smog and rain added their part to the slow progression of the Indian innings, and when Azharuddin refused to declare, even when India had batted until lunch on the fourth day and reached 417 for seven, the crowd started to vent their frustration. Fruit was thrown onto the pitch at the Indian team and punters turned their anger on the Indian captain, to the point where the game was further delayed as the pitch was cleared of debris and the police tried to restore order in the stands. When India eventually declared, Cowans had three for 103 to his name and Edmonds three for 72. Mike Gatting made a solid 48 in England's reply, but unsurprisingly the game ended in a draw. Azharuddin's popularity with the cricket-mad Indian fans was not enhanced any further when England won the fourth Test in Madras and drew the final Test in Kanpur to secure a 2-1 series win. Gatting himself had an exceptional tour, scoring 575 runs at an average of 95.83, including his highest Test score of 207 in the fourth Test.